Supporting the Student Journey into Higher Education

This book will provide an in-depth look at the development, functionality and appeal of pre-arrival platforms to aid transition into higher education, including a range of provisions.

Ensuring a smooth transition into higher education study is increasingly seen as key to both retention and success, both in the initial weeks of study and beyond. Pre-arrival platforms offer students a range of opportunities, which might include the chance to familiarise themselves with the practices and policies of their new institution before teaching begins. This book will explore these platforms from three different angles: their development, use and appeal to diverse audiences in higher education, and case studies illustrating their incorporation into practice. It will provide a comprehensive overview of not only the different ways in which such platforms add value to the transition process but also the way they embrace diversity and widening participation in higher education from the very beginning of an individual's higher education career. With chapters written by individuals from a variety of roles in higher education, this text will also provide the reader an insight into issues arising from the use of these platforms.

It will be essential reading for educational, academic and staff developers working with departments and their institutions to develop their support structure for new students as well as for those directly involved in widening access/participation programmes.

Wendy Garnham is Professor of Psychology at the University of Sussex, UK.

Nina Walker is Associate Professor of Learning and Teaching at the University of Hertfordshire, UK.

The Staff and Educational Development Association Focus Series
Series Editor: Stephen Powell

The SEDA Focus series is for everyone interested in teaching, learning and assessment in higher education. Books in the Series are scholarly and practical, written by educational developers and researchers on up-to-the minute topics, bringing together experience and practice in a theoretical context. The Series is for educational, academic, staff and faculty developers, subject academics developing their professional teaching interests, institutional managers and everyone working to improve the quality of student learning. SEDA (The Staff and Educational Development Association) is the long-established professional association for staff and educational developers in the UK, promoting innovation and good practice in higher education.

Titles in the series:

Supporting the Student Journey into Higher Education
How Pre-Arrival Platforms Can Enhance Widening Participation
Edited by Wendy Garnham and Nina Walker

Perspectives on Teaching and Learning Leadership in Higher Education
Case Studies from UK and Australia
Edited by Josephine Lang, Namrata Rao and Anesa Hosein

Active Learning in Higher Education
Theoretical Considerations and Perspectives
Edited by Wendy Garnham and Isobel Gowers

For more information about this series, please visit: www.routledge.com/SEDA-Focus/book-series/SEDAF

Supporting the Student Journey into Higher Education

How Pre-Arrival Platforms Can
Enhance Widening Participation

Edited by Wendy Garnham and Nina Walker

Routledge
Taylor & Francis Group

LONDON AND NEW YORK

First published 2024
by Routledge
4 Park Square, Milton Park, Abingdon, Oxon OX14 4RN

and by Routledge
605 Third Avenue, New York, NY 10158

Routledge is an imprint of the Taylor & Francis Group, an informa business

© 2024 selection and editorial matter, Wendy Garnham and
Nina Walker; individual chapters, the contributors

The right of Wendy Garnham and Nina Walker to be identified as the authors
of the editorial material, and of the authors for their individual chapters, has
been asserted in accordance with sections 77 and 78 of the Copyright,
Designs and Patents Act 1988.

British Library Cataloguing-in-Publication Data
A catalogue record for this book is available from the British Library

Library of Congress Cataloging-in-Publication Data
Names: Garnham, Wendy, editor. | Walker, Nina, 1969– editor.
Title: Supporting the student journey into higher education : how pre-arrival
    platforms can enhance widening participation / Edited by Wendy A.
    Garnham and Nina Walker.
Description: Abingdon, Oxon ; New York, NY : Routledge, 2024. |
    Series: SEDA focus | Includes bibliographical references and index.
Identifiers: LCCN 2023056660 (print) | LCCN 2023056661 (ebook) |
    ISBN 9781032548036 (hardback) | ISBN 9781032548029 (paperback) |
    ISBN 9781003427575 (ebook)
Subjects: LCSH: College preparation programs—Psychological aspects. |
    College student orientation. | Motivation in education.
Classification: LCC LB2351.2 .S84 2024 (print) | LCC LB2351.2 (ebook) |
    DDC 378.1/610973—dc23/eng/20231221
LC record available at https://lccn.loc.gov/2023056660
LC ebook record available at https://lccn.loc.gov/2023056661

ISBN: 978-1-032-54803-6 (hbk)
ISBN: 978-1-032-54802-9 (pbk)
ISBN: 978-1-003-42757-5 (ebk)

DOI: 10.4324/9781003427575

Typeset in Times New Roman
by Apex CoVantage, LLC

Contents

About the editors

Wendy Garnham is a Professor of Psychology at the University of Sussex and a National Teaching Fellow. As co-founder of the international Active Learning Network, her scholarly interests are dominated by active learning pedagogy. Wendy is a Senior Fellow of Advance HE, a Fellow of SEDA and jointly hosts a regular community of practice for academics interested in Transition into, through and out of higher education. She has edited open access books on active learning as well as a SEDA Special publication on Transitions and contributed a case study to an Advance HE publication on action research. Wendy publishes on a number of blogs including, the SEDA blog and on the Exchange, a University of Sussex blog site as well as the School of Psychology blog.

Nina Walker is an Associate Professor (Learning and Teaching) at the University of Hertfordshire and a National Teaching Fellow. She leads the Transition to Higher Education module, aimed at providing a scaffolded entry to higher education, and she also leads the Institutional approach to Personal tutoring. She is a Senior Fellow of the Higher Education Academy with a keen interest in transitions and her PhD focuses on academic confidence. She is an active member of the SEDA Transitions Community of Practice and has edited the publication Pharmacy OSCES. She is a member of the editorial committee for 100+ Ideas for Active Learning. Nationally she works with the Pharmacy Schools Council Student Success Group to support Master of Pharmacy students across the UK. Her work is shared predominantly through conference presentations and also through the National Teaching Repository. Her experience working with incoming students and also her research and teaching have driven her input in this book.

Contributors

Katherine Kruger is Senior Lecturer in Community Engagement and Lead Academic Success Advisor for the Central Foundation Years Programme at the University of Sussex. Katherine is a specialist in modern and contemporary literature and teaches modules with a practical or experiential component on the Liberal Arts BA at Sussex. In her role with the Foundation Years Programme, she has designed and led a number of projects that focus on inclusive, compassionate advising for student success.

Emily Baker is Lecturer in Music, Film & Media and Academic Success Advisor for the Central Foundation Years Programme at the University of Sussex. She has over 20 years' experience of working in, and then teaching about, music and the creative industries. In 2023, she completed her doctorate in pop music, aging and time. In her role as Academic Success Advisor, her research interests are largely centred around enhancing academic transitions – working with students to find creative ways to examine, critique, (re)frame and ultimately empower them on their academic journeys.

Karen Tucker is the Student Experience Officer for the Central Foundation Years Programme at the University of Sussex. She is particularly interested in EDI and supports students from underrepresented groups.

Neil Ford is Principal Teaching Fellow (Academic Development) in the Centre for Higher Education Practice (CHEP) at the University of Southampton and is passionate about working in partnership with staff and students to improve learning and teaching. His work cuts across the disciplines of education development and learning development and current work includes: faculty liaison, fostering communities of practice in teaching development, development of programme leadership and supporting student transitions. His research interests include partnership between staff and students, enhancing academic transitions, developing structured peer support schemes, teaching development (especially for early career academics) and mentoring (e.g., supporting colleagues to achieve Advance HE recognition).

Becky Lewis is Lecturer in Evolutionary Biology at the University of East Anglia. She also holds administrative roles of Transition Officer and Director of Admissions for the School of Biological Sciences. She is particularly interested in the interactions between student social lives, their well-being and their motivation to study, and she has organised several social events to try to improve engagement with the course. Additionally, she is interested in encouraging educators to share best practice with regard to developing skills in undergraduate students.

Kelly Edmunds is Associate Professor in the School of Biological Sciences at the University of East Anglia. She holds a University Teaching Fellowship and was the 2022 recipient of the Sir Geoffrey and Lady Allen prize for Excellence in Teaching. She has taught in higher education for more than a decade and is currently Deputy Director of Learning and Teaching and Deputy Head of the Teaching Theme as well as Programme Director for the Science Foundation Year courses. She leads a community of practice focused on student belonging and is passionate about ensuring that higher education is accessible to all and that students are encouraged to develop their resilience and self-efficacy to enable them to thrive.

Emma Palmer (FHEA) is Director of Foundation Year at the University of Hull, teaching and supporting Foundation Year students as they transition into and through university. She has been involved in a range of projects over her 11 years of working in higher education, such as a QAA Collaborate Enhancement Project for the University of Hull's Inclusive Education Framework and Toolkit. In 2020, she completed her MA in Education, Inclusion and Special Needs, in which her dissertation reviewed how transition, identities, sense of belonging and communities play a key role in the student journey throughout their time at university.

Fran Garrad-Cole (PFHEA and National Teaching Fellow) is a Psychology Teaching and Scholarship academic and is Deputy Head of School at Bangor University where she teaches across the undergraduate curriculum and has held several teaching administration roles such as Assessment Director, Senior Tutor, Disabilities officer and other roles. She is known for her innovation and, in her role as a Teaching and Learning Developer in Bangor University's Centre for Enhancement of Learning and teaching (CELT), has designed and led several institutional projects to address common issues such as student retention, engagement, reassessment and transition. One such project was a four-part transitions and induction project designed to better understand and support incoming students to the University particularly in the context of COVID-19. The project is comprised of the following elements : a Be Bangor Ready pre-arrival website providing high-level information and support for students considering studying at Bangor University; a pre-arrival questionnaire capturing the educational experiences and upcoming interests and concerns of incoming students to provide context for transition support; an adjustment to exam assessment for first-year students such that exams are minimised in semester 1 and supported with formative assessment in semester 2 and a year-long self-directed online induction module providing timely support for induction throughout the first year at university.

Laura Boubert is Chartered Psychologist and Principal Lecturer in Cognitive Psychology at the University of Westminster, where she is Course Leader for the BSc in Cognitive and Clinical Neuroscience. She leads modules exploring cognitive psychology for undergraduate and postgraduate students alongside her research on student transitions and brain injury and cognitive disorders. Being a senior fellow of the Higher Education Academy, she has always been passionate about developing students' academic skills so that they can make the most of their time at university and showcase their subject-based knowledge. She has designed and delivered academic skills resources and workshops for over 20 years and is a member of several higher education (HE) groups focusing on how we can support students to transition into HE as successfully as possible.

James Fenton is Senior Lecturer at the University of Westminster. He currently lectures in Academic English at the Centre for Education and Teaching Innovation. He has over 25 years' experience of English language teaching in 11 countries and has previously lectured in Language Acquisition and Clinical Linguistics in UK higher education. His recent published research explores multilingual language assessment and access to education.

Victoria Wilson-Crane has over 25 years' experience of working in education in formal and non-formal settings. For 16 of those years, she has been working for Kaplan International and is currently Senior Director of Innovative Student Learning. She leads the Centre for Learning Innovation and Quality, a team of 20 leaders and developers across quality assurance and enhancement, learning measurement and evaluation and learning design. She holds a Ph.D. in Lifelong Learning, which explored the experiences of young people in transition from school to further education. She is Fellow of Advance HE and Senior Fellow of the Staff and Educational Development Association.

Hengyi Wang (FHEA) is Senior Student Academic Success Advisor at the University of Sussex Business School. Over the past 10 years, since travelling from mainland China to the UK to study for a degree programme, she has been supporting international students through all stages of their university journeys. As an academic success advisor, where more than 30% of students are Chinese, she has developed a strong link with the Chinese international student community. She also works as the Equality, Diversity and Inclusion (EDI) Champion in the Business School, responsible for the School's EDI initiatives. Prior to her current role, she has worked as an International Support Advisor for foundation year, international year one and degree course students. Her professional and personal experiences have given her in-depth insight into how universities can best support international students through their transition into UK HE.

Sarah Watson is an academic developer at Sussex, where she supports international student transition. This responsibility draws upon her previous experiences of working closely with international students as a pre-sessional tutor at the University of Southampton and her support of international student transition at the University of Roehampton. Before becoming an Academic Developer, she worked as a student academic success advisor, providing support to a largely international student community. Her preliminary studies into the potential barriers to learning for non-EU students in the University of Sussex Business School (USBS) were presented at the School's Teaching and Learning Conference. Extending this work, she became the co-recipient of both a British Academy Small Research Grant and the Warwick International Higher Education Academy External Collaboration Fund. Both funds help develop research into, and resources to support, the international student experience in UK HE.

Rebecca Wilson is a student development professional at the University of St Andrews and holds a PhD in International Relations. She has practical experience of lecturing and tutoring students, as well as specialising in the transition of students into the University, including expertise in mentoring, study skills and the award-winning pre-arrival platform: the 'Transitions Toolkit'.

Steve Russell has been working at Aston University for 20 years in both Pharmacy and now Bioscience teaching on several different programmes from our Foundation in science program to Masters level. He is part of the physiology teaching team, personal tutor and the biology lead for the foundation program. He has a Masters in Education and is Fellow of Advance HE.

Peter Alston is Associate Professor of Educational Practice and Dean of Education Services at BPP University. He has a background in information systems and web development & programming, and he holds a doctorate in e-research and technology enhanced learning. He has worked in higher education for the past 18 years in a number of public/private universities across undergraduate, postgraduate & apprenticeship provision, working collaboratively with colleagues across multiple disciplines to enhance curriculum design/delivery and the student experience. His scholarly interests lie in electronic assessment (specifically the implications for policy and practice in HE), the use of technology to support teaching and learning and the student transition to higher education.

Dawne Irving-Bell is Professor of Learning and Teaching at BPP University, UK. She is a National Teaching Fellow, Principal Fellow of the Higher Education Academy, holds a Collaborative Award for Teaching Excellence and received a National Award in recognition of her outstanding contribution to Teacher Education. With a passion for visual-thinking and technology education, she established The National Teaching Repository an Open Education Resource with proven reach and impact across the global higher education community. She is an editor-in-chief of the *Journal of Social-Media for Learning* and through her work within the International Society for the Scholarship of Teaching and Learning (ISSOTL) is committed to raising the profile of the Scholarship of Teaching and Learning.

Sarah McIlroy is the Dean of International Higher Education and Dean of the Business School at BPP University. She has responsibility for the University International and DNA strategy and has a proven track record in designing and developing innovative education solutions to meet the needs of students who look to the UK for practical programmes which enable them to develop demonstrable employability skills. She is an accomplished conference speaker engaging with professional bodies and employers in the UK and globally and is an advocate for the ongoing UK International Higher Education Strategy. She is committed to sharing best practice across the sector on the benefits of investing in supporting international inbound students to achieve their potential.

Claire Stocks is Associate Professor of Educational Practice within the Learning and Teaching team at BPP University. She has worked as an academic developer for the last 18 years, after completing a doctorate in American Literature at Keele University. She has a particular interest in supporting the development of novice academics, whether they are doctoral students who teach or dual professionals who have moved into academic roles from practice or industry backgrounds. She has been a Senior Fellow of Advance HE since 2016 and has presented and published in the areas of both American Literature and Academic Development.

David Wooff is Associate Professor of Educational Practice, and Director of Apprenticeship Quality and Compliance for BPP University. He is a Fellow of the Charted College of Teaching (FCCT), the Society of Education and Training (FCET) and the Royal Society for Arts (FRSA) and a Senior Fellow of the Higher Education Academy (SFHEA). He holds the position of Chair of the National Teaching Repository. He has widely published in the fields of technology education and teacher training. His current interests lie in the Scholarship of Teaching and Learning (SoTL) and the impact and benefit of apprenticeships and work-based learning.

Adam Paxman is Academic Skills Advisor with the Student Engagement team at Edge Hill University. Adam provides academic skills and information skills guidance to undergraduate and taught postgraduate students through both face-to-face and virtual 1–2–1 appointments, face-to-face or virtual embedded sessions and face-to-face workshops or webinars. His role also includes a specific focus on induction and transitions. He previously taught and supported learning in further education, worked as a freelance illustrator and, while lecturing in higher education, specialised in contextual studies for several undergraduate design disciplines.

Kathy Egea leads the First and Further Experience (FFYE) Program at the University of Technology Sydney (UTS) and is Senior Lecturer in the Teaching and Curriculum Team (TACT) within the central T&L unit. In enabling a whole of university approach to student transition success, her passion is to connect, link, draw on practice and build communities of those passionate about the student transition experience, in both curricular and co-curricular spaces. The FFYE program (formerly FYE) engages a huge community of academics, professional staff and some students to share, learn and connect through grants and forums to support. The program has won national recognition through OLT citation (2016), finalist in 2021 CAULLT Global Good Practice Award. Kathy co-leads the FYE national Australasian Network for STARS (see unistars.org) and was awarded the 2021 STARS Fellow for her work in creating the conditions for practice change around student transition.

Katie Padilla is the manager of Global Mobility Programmes Inbound for UTS International. She has 19 years of professional experience in international education, living and working in various countries including, France, Germany, Spain, the UK, Argentina and Australia. She has a strong passion for developing exchange programmes which are sustainable, inclusive, welcoming and accessible to a diverse group of students and is currently responsible for managing the Inbound Study Abroad and Exchange program at UTS.

Jason Do is an Engaged Learning Coordinator who has been working in the student engagement area for 5 years at the University of Technology Sydney, Faculty of Engineering and IT. He leads the design, delivery and ongoing support of student engagement initiatives and projects in his faculty with the aim to increase student satisfaction, success, retention and well-being. His initiatives involve working together with student leaders, cohort focused programmes and first and further year experience projects in the teaching and learning space.

Deanna Horvath is Senior Lecturer in the School of Allied Health, Human Services and Sport at La Trobe University in Melbourne. She is passionate about supporting first-year students and has been teaching large first-year subjects across health at different Victorian universities for over 15 years. She has received an Australian Award for University Teaching (AAUT) Citation for her work in developing programmes to support student transition and success. She is interested in university preparation programmes, transition, the first-year experience and the use of technology in online learning design.

Christopher Bridge is a Research Fellow in teaching innovation at La Trobe University and the University of New England. He has worked extensively in learning and teaching since 2004, including in international student support; academic skills development; supplemental instruction; internationalisation of the curriculum; assurance of learning; student success, transition and retention; teaching technologies including 360 video, teaching with a tablet computer, and 3D animation; personalising the student experience using learning analytics; and in supporting skills development in teaching academics through communities of practice and practice-sharing. His current research investigates generative AI in higher education.

Michelle Morgan is a national and internationally recognised Student Experience Transitions Specialist across all levels of study and is extensively published in the area. She is currently Dean of Students at the University of East London. She is a Principal Fellow of the HEA, Fellow of the AUA, an elected council member of UKCGE and Student Minds Mental Health Charter Assessor. During her varied career, she has been a faculty manager, lecturer, researcher and academic manager. She describes herself as a 'Third Space Integrated Student Experience Practitioner' who develops initiatives based on pragmatic and practical research. She has more than 50 publications and has presented more than 100 national and international conference papers (including 52 keynotes and 30 invited papers). She has developed a free portal for staff which provides a range of information and links for anyone interested in improving the student experience in higher education www.improvingthestudentexperience.com. She was creator and PI/Project Lead of an innovative, £2.7 million, 11 university collaborative HEFCE grant, looking at the study expectations and attitudes of postgraduate taught (PGT) students. The project contributed evidence that introduced the PG Loan Scheme.

Introduction

Nina Walker

The transition to university can be an exciting but also potentially anxiety-provoking time where support may be needed (Morosanu et al., 2010). The literature exploring the initial transition period has burgeoned, with abundant evidence as to how to best support students (Briggs et al., 2012; Perander et al., 2021; Thomas, 2013). However, the relationship a student has with their university starts potentially far earlier than the transition period.

There is no standardised definition of when the pre-arrival period stems from and to, but within the confines of this book, the pre-arrival period is taken to be from the point of confirmation of an offer to study, to arrival at university. Throughout this book, the authors are, however, mindful of the impact that the pre-arrival period can have on onward transition.

Arguably, traditional induction is perhaps no longer fit for purpose, when students are now required to be conversant with an increasing volume of information, while likely working to support themselves, with some adopting caring roles in addition to studying. As a result, pre-arrival support is fast becoming an essential part of a university's arsenal for effective, accessible student support, helping to scaffold, acclimatise and develop incoming students. As our student bodies continue to diversify, institutions need to keep pace by pro-actively supporting these students, especially those with many intersecting characteristics.

Pre-arrival platforms are online web-based resources which are used in various ways to support students in the pre-arrival period and, also in some cases, in the early transition phase. These platforms have evolved from providing basic information for example with regard to registration, visa queries or orientation, to complex interactive environments where students can, for example, interact virtually, secure study skills, get to know staff, experience webinars and enhance their sense of belonging. The proliferation of mechanisms used has garnered an increased focus on the effective use of platforms, which can then be targeted at the module, programme or institution level and vary in terms of their formality, reach and target audience.

DOI: 10.4324/9781003427575-1

The importance of engaging students at this early stage in the student academic lifecycle has been highlighted by Thomas (2013). Thomas also noted that students historically received insufficient information about a range of aspects of higher education, arrive underprepared and with unrealistic expectations. All of these factors have the potential to impact the willingness of students to persist at university. Therefore, a focus on the pre-arrival phase is important to both the student body and the institution.

The propagation of pre-arrival platforms has likely been accelerated by worldwide events such as the COVID pandemic, forcing higher education institutions to adapt their provision for supporting students. Staff had to pivot rapidly online to familiarise students with processes and structures associated with university life. The pandemic curveball also played havoc with the knowledge acquisition of many students (Turner et al., 2020). Acknowledging the potential impact of the pandemic on students, Smith (2022) utilised a pre-arrival questionnaire adapted from Morgan (2020) to direct support for incoming students affected by the pandemic. Smith (2022) identified that 'over half of those in study at school or college had not been engaged in structured learning for over six months before starting their university' (p5), with over a third of respondents worried about coping with the level of study. These stark statistics pointed to a need for additional scaffolding of study skills in the pre-arrival period, with Wingate (2007) suggesting that this critical time period provides the opportunity to increase student preparedness.

Platforms often aim to better scaffold student development; however, scarce consideration in the literature has been given to the design and creation of platforms, especially for discrete groups of students, such as those who identify as Widening Participation students. The importance of widening participation as a concept has been long established, certainly since the Robbins Report (1963), and remains of contemporary importance as evidenced through the strategic implementation of Action and Participation Plans (OfS, 2023). This means it is imperative that we ensure that our attention is turned to providing good-quality pre-arrival support. Achieving this is a multifaceted task; however, acute support in the pre-arrival period offers the chance to provide incoming students with additional support for learning, development of skills and academic confidence (Sander & Sanders, 2009), which may in turn help secure their self-belief and progress in tertiary study.

The outcomes of the introduction of a quality pre-arrival platform are manifold but, importantly, most aim to enhance the sense of belonging. *What works* (Thomas, 2012) illustrated the need for a focus on belonging and 'mattering' for students, suggesting that if students develop a sense of belonging, they tend to achieve higher grades. In the report 'Building Belonging in Higher Education' created by Pearson and Wonkhe (Blake et al., 2022), development of a sense of belonging was clearly associated with Connections, Inclusion, Support and Autonomy, all of which can be stimulated through the use of carefully considered pre-arrival platforms. Indeed, the report gives specific mention to the value that pre-arrival surveys can make on the sense of belonging.

As student demographics are in flux, as a sector we are pushed to develop fluid mechanisms that best support our student body. Increasingly imposter syndrome (Clance & Imes, 1978) has been recognised as a factor which impacts students in a variety of ways; for example, imposter syndrome is negatively associated with happiness (Pákozdy et al., 2023). Hewertson and Tissa (2022) also note that imposter syndrome disproportionally affects marginalised groups. Pre-arrival platforms, however, may have the potential to meaningfully impact students and help to allay feelings of 'imposterism' through activities such as peer mentoring, early conversation with peers and staff, and expectation setting, for example.

Alongside belonging as a key driver, co-creation is also clearly articulated as a positive step in the development of pre-arrival platforms. The value of student partnership is well documented in the literature (Healey & Healey, 2019; Bovill et al., 2011), and it is pleasing to see how many universities have identified the power of working with students as partners (Neary et al., 2014). As you work your way through this book, this theme and the positive effects of working with students as partners will emerge.

So how was this publication created? The SEDA Transitions Community of Practice actively seeks to share good practice around supporting students across the differing transitions associated with higher education study. Within the community, it was noted that the literature on the positive impacts of pre-arrival platforms is growing; however, there is a scarcity of insights into the practicalities of establishing such platforms and the diversity of ways in which platforms are utilised. Through discussion, this led to the concept of this practical, initiative-based book. Chapters have been created by members of the community with specialist interest in supporting students especially in the pre-arrival period. They bring real-life experiences, practical tips and encouragement in the creation of mechanisms to support students in this crucial period.

This publication is designed to particularly encourage the development of platforms to support Widening Participation, aiming to do this by exploring a range of practice which exists within the community. This is undertaken through three broad aspects. Initially, we consider the development of pre-arrival platforms.

In Chapter 1, Wendy Garnham, Katherine Kruger, Emily Baker and Karen Tucker take us through key practicalities when setting up a pre-arrival platform, highlighting the impact of collaborative working between professional and teaching staff in the platform creation. This chapter also explores the benefits of general and discipline-specific information in the pre-arrival period.

Neil Ford explores the importance of working collaboratively with students as partners in the creation, evaluation and enhancement of pre-arrival platforms. Chapter 2 also outlines the benefits this approach derives for the institution and the students, supported through a case study illustrating key aspects.

Chapter 3 provides an honest review of the barriers and challenges encountered when setting up a pre-arrival platform. Through Kelly Edmund and Becky Lewis' experience, we observe the evolution of Preparing for your Studies, a module designed to support students in the pre-arrival period, from its predecessor the Transitions Toolkit. Kelly and Becky adopted an interdisciplinary approach to development of the platform, which is designed to enhance confidence in academic skills and also help to build a sense of community within the incoming students.

Part II then explores the use of pre-arrival platforms. These four chapters explore pre-arrival platforms via differing lenses.

Emma Palmer guides us through ways to foster a sense of belonging using pre-arrival platforms in Chapter 4. Using a fictional case study, Emma encourages the reader to examine student characteristics that might affect the pre-arrival experience, in the context of belonging, identity and community. Potential solutions to some of these barriers are offered, and the reader is also given the opportunity to review their own practice to find ways to enhance these important aspects for their incoming students.

Chapter 5 highlights how you can use a pre-arrival platform as part of an induction programme. Fran Garrad-Cole talks of her experiences using a pre-arrival platform to help familiarise students with university mechanisms and processes, with an aim to cement early confidence and support retention within higher education.

Laura Boubert and James Fenton discuss the development of skills training via pre-arrival platforms. Acknowledging that university study can be very different to that of school or college, Chapter 6 helps bridge this gap and shares examples of what skills training can be stored and delivered via a pre-arrival platform.

In Chapter 7, Victoria Wilson-Crane examines how pre-arrival platforms can help students to consider engagement with career provision within the pre-arrival period, developing employability skills from this early stage. Reflections showcase the impact of this exciting initiative.

In Part III, we aim to reflect the diversity of students within higher education and explore pre-arrival platforms which are designed with a specific student demographic in mind.

Sarah Watson and Hengyi Wang direct our attention in Chapter 8 to consider how a pre-arrival platform can support international students develop a sense of belonging with the co-creation of bilingual welcome packs.

In Chapter 9, Rebecca Wilson explores the role of pre-arrival platforms as part of expectation setting for new students through offering an opportunity for critical self-reflection for students in advance of undertaking study and providing a mechanism for feedback from students.

Steve Russell takes us on a journey to explore how pre-arrival platforms can help the smooth transition for mature, often also non-traditional students. This chapter actively explores how to best support students with many competing identities.

In Chapter 11, Peter Alston, Dawne Irving-Bell, Sarah McIlroy, Claire Stocks and David Wooff showcase the benefit of utilising a pre-arrival platform to support non-traditional students. A selection of case studies allows us to explore the impact that considered support in the early phase can have.

Adam Paxman illustrates how Getting Started with UniSkills, a series of webinars, can assist postgraduate students in the return to study within higher education. The webinars cover bespoke skills, helping to enhance confidence and belonging.

In the final chapter, Kathy Egea, Katie Padilla, Jason Do, Deanna Harvath and Christopher Bridge introduce us to concepts underpinning the use of pre-arrival platforms in Australia, exploring a series of activities aimed at international and equity-disadvantaged students.

While each chapter discusses a stand-alone topic, they all relate to each other through the central theme. Feel free to dip into specific topics or work your way through the entire book to give an overview of the practicalities to consider when developing a pre-arrival platform, their use and appeal to diverse populations within higher education.

In conclusion, this publication is intended to fuel readers' interest in the impact that pre-arrival support can have on the widening participation contingent. As pre-arrival platforms secure a place of greater standing within the sector, these insights are hoped to help trigger the instigation or cementing of a more conscious effort supporting students in this liminal period.

References

Blake, S., Capper, G., & Jackson, A. (2022). Building belonging in higher education: Recommendations for developing an integrated institutional approach. *Pearson & WonkHE*, 1–41.

Bovill, C., Cook-Sather, A., & Felten, P. (2011). Students as co-creators of teaching approaches, course design, and curricula: Implications for academic developers. *International Journal for Academic Development*, *16*(2), 133–145.

Briggs, A. R., Clark, J., & Hall, I. (2012). Building bridges: Understanding student transition to university. *Quality in Higher Education*, *18*(1), 3–21.

Clance, P. R., & Imes, S. A. (1978). The imposter phenomenon in high achieving women: Dynamics and therapeutic intervention. *Psychotherapy: Theory, Research & Practice*, *15*(3), 241.

Healey, M., & Healey, R. L. (2019). *Student engagement through partnership: A guide and Update to the advance HE framework (04)*. Advance HE.

Hewertson, H., & Tissa, F. (2022). Intersectional imposter syndrome: How imposterism affects marginalised groups. In *The Palgrave handbook of imposter syndrome in higher education* (pp. 19–35). Springer International Publishing.

Morgan, M. (2020). *Bridging the gap between secondary and tertiary education.* www.improvingthestudentexperience.com/library/UG_documents/Bridging_the_gap_between_secondary_and_tertiary_education-Morgan_2020.pdf

Morosanu, L., Handley, K., & O'Donovan, B. (2010). Seeking support: Researching first-year students' experiences of coping with academic life. *Higher Education Research & Development, 29*(6), 665–678.

Neary, M., Saunders, G., Hagyard, A., & Derricott, D. (2014). *Student as producer: Research-engaged teaching, an institutional strategy.* Higher Education Academy.

Office for Students. (2023). *Access and participation plans.* [Internet]. Retrieved October 28, 2023, from https://officeforstudents.org.uk/advice-and-guidance/promoting-equal-opportunities/access-and-participation-plans/

Pákozdy, C., Askew, J., Dyer, J., Gately, P., Martin, L., Mavor, K. I., & Brown, G. R. (2023). The imposter phenomenon and its relationship with self-efficacy, perfectionism and happiness in university students. *Current Psychology*, 1–10.

Perander, K., Londen, M., & Holm, G. (2021). Supporting students' transition to higher education. *Journal of Applied Research in Higher Education, 13*(2), 622–632.

Robbins, L. R. B. (1963). *Higher education: Report of the committee appointed by the prime minister under the chairmanship of Lord Robbins, 1961–63* (Vol. 1, No. 5). HM Stationery Office.

Sander, P., & Sanders, L. (2009). Measuring academic behavioural confidence: The ABC scale revisited. *Studies in Higher Education, 34*(1), 19–35.

Smith, S. (2022). Entry to university at a time of COVID-19: How using a pre-arrival academic questionnaire informed support for new first-year students at Leeds Beckett University. *AISHE-J: The All Ireland Journal of Teaching and Learning in Higher Education, 14*(2), 1–23.

Thomas, L. (2012). Building student engagement and belonging in Higher Education at a time of change. *Paul Hamlyn Foundation, 100*(1–99).

Thomas, L. (2013). What works? Facilitating an effective transition into higher education. *Widening Participation and Lifelong Learning, 14*(1), 4–24.

Turner, K. L., Hughes, M., & Presland, K. (2020). Learning loss, a potential challenge for transition to undergraduate study following COVID19 school disruption. *Journal of Chemical Education, 97*(9), 3346–3352.

Wingate, U. (2007). A framework for transition: Supporting 'learning to learn' in higher education. *Higher Education Quarterly, 61*(3), 391–405.

Part I

The development of pre-arrival platforms

1 The practicalities of creating a pre-arrival platform

Wendy Garnham, Katherine Kruger, Emily Baker and Karen Tucker

What did we ever do without a pre-arrival platform (PAP)? It is a question that many institutions in the sector might consider now that these have become more commonplace. However, prior to 2019, students joining the Central Foundation Programmes at the University of Sussex did not have access to such a platform. Induction week was an action-packed extravaganza of information about everything from how to access timetables to what support was available to module introductions. The result was that students were frequently overwhelmed with information, much of which was then later repeated. This is not an isolated experience. Ecclestone et al. (2009) point to the way in which transition can often be:

... unsettling, difficult and unproductive ...

(p. 2).

Leese (2010) points to the heightened stress at this time. Trying to find a way to address these challenges has led to the development of a variety of pre-arrival platforms that enable students to engage with relevant material and information in a more leisurely fashion in the lead-up to the start of their course.

Since its creation in 2019, the pre-arrival platform for the Central Foundation Programmes at the University of Sussex has become a critical part of the support offered to students joining us. Not only does the platform allow students to access information about their course before coming to campus but it has been developed to extend right through from pre-arrival to completion of the foundation year supporting students not just in what to expect from their course but also in finding housemates for the following year, becoming a student rep and even managing their time effectively.

It is easy to think that such a resource is simple and quick to establish particularly as pre-arrival platforms are now well established but for anyone setting up or developing such a platform, the practicalities can often reveal hidden challenges and hurdles. In this chapter, we seek to share some of the experiences we have had in the hope that these might prove useful and informative for those working in transition.

DOI: 10.4324/9781003427575-3

The practicalities of setting up a pre-arrival platform

Key decisions to be made

In setting up a pre-arrival platform, a number of decisions have to be made early on. These include:

- Where to host the platform? Students often do not have access to virtual learning environments (VLEs) until they register but it is important to give students a chance to familiarise themselves with the same resources they will be accessing during their studies.
- What content to make available on the platform? A fine balance has to be struck between making key content available and not overwhelming students. Decisions have to be made about what information is useful and timely.
- How to deliver that content? We know from Long (2009) that students are often reluctant to read large bodies of text due to finding this challenging. However, using a variety of modes of delivery can prove technologically difficult and require the skill sets of a number of individuals in different roles.

How we addressed these decisions in our PAP?

The pre-arrival platform created at Sussex was designed using the virtual learning environment (Canvas) that students would be expected to access and use throughout their studies. This decision meant that students were immediately introduced to the VLE on registration, but before arriving on campus.

Deciding what information to put on the platform was a much more time-consuming part of the process. As well as general information about support and services available to students, we wanted to be able to share information about the different module options that students could choose from. This not only gave students a chance to consider the different options available to them but also gave professional services staff a chance to register students onto the appropriate modules earlier, reducing the overloading of admin that accompanies the start of a new term.

To achieve this, it was necessary to secure buy-in from module convenors to create information for the pre-arrival platform relating to their own modules. Short introductions and starter activities were collected from module convenors. In the initial pre-arrival platform, brief information about each module option was provided in text form with an idea for an activity that students could try to give them a flavour of what was likely to happen on that module. In later variations, these text blocks were replaced with videos. A member of the professional services team videoed each module convenor introducing their module, the assessments used on that module and the sort of topics covered. It therefore gave students a snapshot of information about the module. There is increasing evidence that students attend more to information in videos (Lin et al., 2022) and that video presentation can support comprehension of information, especially for struggling students (Castek et al., 2009). It does, however, require someone who is familiar and confident with video technology to enable this to occur. More recently, animations have been used alongside traditional videos showing the diverse way that video technology can be used.

As well as module content information, academic success advisors created information Padlet walls giving information about moving to campus and links to welcome week timetables. In recent iterations of the platform, content is being transformed into activities, quizzes and self-study videos with tasks (such as treasure hunts to structure student exploration of the city, instead of suggestions of exhibitions and events), building on research that suggests that interactive content is a beneficial avenue for encouraging more sustained and proactive engagement from students (e.g. Venton & Pompano, 2021).

Importance of a collaborative process

Designing and continually developing a pre-arrival platform is not a light undertaking. It requires the collaboration of individuals from a range of roles, from student experience teams, to academic developers, to faculty. As Solomon (2013) suggests:

> Communication between key stakeholders . . . is the key . . .
>
> (p. 83)

Such communication can facilitate decision-making around what content to use. For example, while faculty may have an idea of common questions that arise within their own modules, it is only through collaboration with professional services staff that more general queries can be identified and addressed on the platform. In the Foundation Year PAP, the professional services team devised a set of frequently asked questions that formed the basis for a quick reference guide for the platform. As the platform developed, students' experienced colleagues contributed their knowledge of notable pressure points for students across the year so that relevant and timely support information could be released at appropriate times.

There can, however, be a chasm between knowing *what* to put on a PAP and knowing *how* to do this. One of the biggest hurdles for professionals trying to develop new learning resources is a technical skills deficit (see Michael, 2007 for a discussion of barriers to active learning). We experienced difficulties in creating interactive material for the PAP, particularly with creating videos. To overcome this obstacle, academic developers and learning technologists played a vital role, advising on different technological elements of the delivery.

Advantages of having a comprehensive site

PAPs are for most students the first point at which they can familiarise themselves with the requirements of university study. Having a site that gives students access to comprehensive resources beginning at pre-arrival and into the first year is essential to ensuring retention of students (MacFarlane, 2019) and to allaying student anxieties (Woods & Homer, 2022). It can serve as a central location for all student queries and act as a single communication point for staff to contact all students.

In discussion with colleagues nationally about transition practice (in particular, Fran Garrad-Cole; see Chapter 5), the PAP used in the Central Foundation Year has now been integrated into a canvas site called the Hub, which gives students ongoing tasks and information designed to support transitions throughout the year by revealing relevant weekly content at particular moments in the student journey. Releasing material incrementally in this way takes account of transition as a continuous process rather than a moment in time. It means that we are able to pre-empt particular pressure points, such as home sickness in week 4 of term, by setting the task in week 3 of scheduling a meeting with Academic Advisor. Araújo et al. (2014) describe the transition into higher education as not so much of an 'event' as a 'process' and the extension of pre-arrival activities through induction and into the first year of study offers a chance to illustrate this to our students.

Having this information unfolding for the whole cohort each week also normalises and contextualises what might otherwise be isolating thoughts, feelings or experiences. This is particularly important for international students who may arrive late to campus, potentially missing the pre-arrival activities completely. With a comprehensive site such as the Hub, this information is readily available and accessible at all times, providing a reference point and information source that helps to allay anxieties in transition.

Inclusivity in design

Kift and Nelson (2005) argue that to successfully support students in transitioning to higher education, universities must acknowledge and respond to the diversity of the student body. For example, Clerehan (2003) and Yorke and Thomas (2003) have pointed to the challenging nature of induction for particular groups of students, namely first-generation attenders and those from disadvantaged backgrounds, and Shepherd (2022) considers the experience of individuals with autism in transition to be even more destabilising than for most. Sefotho and Onyishi (2021), for example, suggest that students with autism find organizational tasks particularly challenging. In addressing the needs of these diverse student groups, O'Shea (2016) warns against using transition methods to simply 'fill students up' with institutional cultural capital. Rather, we should be drawing upon the experiences of these individuals to help shape transition practice.

In designing the PAP, we wanted to ensure that such groups would be able to access key information that would provide them with a greater sense of confidence about the induction process. We incorporated information on time management and links to various digital tools that could be used to aid this. Information about academic support was provided, and information about mentoring was provided.

An essential part of being able to effectively address the needs of a diverse study body is to incorporate student views and experiences into the design process. For example, feedback from Race Equity Advocates (a team of students of colour employed by the FY Programme to gather feedback from other students on issues around race equality) highlighted the lack of welcome resources tailored specifically to students from racialised minority backgrounds. Responding to this feedback, we incorporated a section on the Hub with resources on race equality for all students to access before starting their studies. These resources include guidance on appropriate language, where to go for support, how to report hate crimes or feedback informally on instances such as microaggressions.

Getting a student's-eye view of the site, co-creating the content with students and making that student involvement clear on the site could make the content more relevant and meaningful to students' experiences and encourage them to continue accessing the site throughout the year, not just during pre-arrival.

The practicalities of creating the pre-arrival platform are an ongoing consideration. Burke et al. (2016) suggest that nurturing trust, a sense of belonging and inclusion are key to supporting the capability of students. Developing a pre-arrival platform that has this at its heart will hopefully be a first step in that direction.

References

Araújo, N., Carlin, D., Clarke, B., Morieson, L., Lukas, K., & Wilson, R. (2014). Belonging in the first year: A creative discipline cohort case study. *International Journal of the First Year in Higher Education, 5*(2).

Burke, P. J., Bennett, A., Burgess, C., Gray, K., & Southgate, E. (2016). *Capability, belonging and equity in higher education: Developing inclusive approaches*. Newcastle, NSW: Centre of Excellence for Equity in Higher Education, The University of Newcastle.

Castek, J., Zawilinski, L., McVerry, J. G., O'Byrne, W. I., & Leu, D. J. (2009). The new literacies of online reading comprehension: New opportunities and challenges for students with learning difficulties. In C. Wyatt-Smith, J. Elkins, & S. Gunn (Eds.), *Multiple perspectives on difficulties in learning literacy and numeracy* (pp. 91–110). Routledge.

Clerehan, R. (2003). Transition to tertiary education in the arts and humanities: Some academic initiatives from Australia. *Arts and Humanities in Higher Education, 2*(1), 72–89.

Ecclestone, K., Biesta, G., & Hughes, M. (2009). Transitions in the lifecourse: The role of identity, agency and structure. In *Transitions and learning through the lifecourse* (pp. 25–39). Routledge.

Kift, S., & Nelson, K. (2005, January). Beyond curriculum reform: Embedding the transition experience. In *Proceedings of the 28th HERDSA annual conference: Higher education in a changing world (HERDSA 2005)*. University of Southern Queensland.

Leese, M. (2010). Bridging the gap: Supporting student transitions into higher education. *Journal of Further and Higher Education, 34*(2), 239–251.

Lin, C. H., Wu, W. H., & Lee, T. N. (2022). Using an online learning platform to show students' achievements and attention in the video lecture and online practice learning environments. *Educational Technology & Society, 25*(1), 155–165.

Long, T. L. (2009). Rescuing reading at the community college. *Inquiry, 14*(1), 5–14.

MacFarlane, K. (2019). Widening participation through the learner life cycle. *Widening Participation and Lifelong Learning, 21*(1), 94–116.

Michael, J. (2007). Faculty perceptions about barriers to active learning. *College Teaching, 55*(2), 42–47.

O'Shea, S. (2016). Avoiding the manufacture of 'sameness': First-in-family students, cultural capital and the higher education environment. *Higher Education, 72*, 59–78.

Sefotho, M. M., & Onyishi, C. N. (2021). Transition to higher education for students with autism: Challenges and support needs. *International Journal of Higher Education, 10*(1), 201–213.

Shepherd, J. (2022). Beyond tick-box transitions? Experiences of autistic students moving from special to further education. *International Journal of Inclusive Education, 26*(9), 878–892.

Solomon, L. (2013). Pre-arrival. In M. Morgan (Ed.), *Supporting student diversity in higher education: A practical guide* (pp. 83–103). Routledge.

Venton, B. J., & Pompano, R. R. (2021). Strategies for enhancing remote student engagement through active learning. *Analytical and Bioanalytical Chemistry, 413*, 1507–1512.

Woods, K., & Homer, D. (2022). The staff–student co-design of an online resource for pre-arrival arts and humanities students. *Arts and Humanities in Higher Education, 21*(2), 176–197.

Yorke, M., & Thomas, L. (2003). Improving the retention of students from lower socio-economic groups. *Journal of Higher Education Policy and Management, 25*(1), 63–74.

2 Student partnership in the development of pre-arrival resources

Neil Ford

More than a decade has passed since the publication of the final report from the 'What Works? Student Retention and Success' programme (Thomas, 2012). Key evidence-based findings from the project suggested that the development of *belonging* is critical to student success and that this is best developed through

> mainstream activities that all students participate in
>
> (Thomas, 2012, p. 6).

The past decade has been a hugely dynamic time in UK higher education. Government policy for a more liberal market economy for higher education, including the removal of student number controls, has resulted in volatility and redistribution of student numbers (Hillman, 2014). We have also lived through 'unprecedented' disruption brought about by the COVID-19 pandemic. Although there is a trend towards more learner-centred approaches focused on student partnership and co-creation (Healey et al., 2014), opportunities to engage with students have been severely disrupted by the 'online pivot' and there are signs that disruption to learning at secondary and tertiary levels may affect the ways that students engage with higher education for some time (Tilak & Kumar, 2022).

This chapter explores the development of an online pre-arrival module at a large Russell Group university (University of Southampton). This chapter will focus on the ways that student partnership and co-creation can be employed to overcome the challenges described above. We will reflect on effective methods for working with student interns, with reference to the post-pandemic shift to online working.

The importance of online pre-arrival modules in transition support

Student lifecycle approaches suggest that the entire *first-year experience* is critical to student success, and experiences in the period between recruitment

DOI: 10.4324/9781003427575-4

and arrival can be extremely formative in the development of students' sense of belonging and expectations of what it is like to study at university (Morgan, 2013). Pre-arrival can be particularly important for underrepresented student groups. Ironically, those with the greatest need to develop belonging and identity (for example 'first-generation students' or international students) often have fewer opportunities to visit in person (Woods & Homer, 2022). *Online* pre-arrival resources are, therefore, a valuable tool in addressing diverse student transition needs while also enhancing the transition to study at university for *all* students (Foster, 2011).

Improving transition: the 'transition project'

Like many institutions, The University of Southampton (UoS) has taken a strategic approach to developing transition support for students. '*Southampton Year 1 – transition into HE*' was a strategic major project established in 2018 to ensure that transition support was developed across the whole institution and was embedded in business-as-usual beyond the project lifecycle. The project was strongly influenced by the 'What Works' reports with a strong focus on developing student identity and belonging, improving student access to support, and enhancing students' academic expectations of studying at university aligned to Thomas's model for student success and retention (Thomas, 2012).

Student partnership has been a critical approach of the project, for example a student co-lead was recruited and was a key member of the project team from project initiation, co-chairing project meetings and boards, and leading on project workstreams. The project also employed several groups of summer interns to deliver on specific, co-created resources supporting effective transition. Outputs of the project that are now embedded in business-as-usual included: influencing the establishment of annual, university-wide, task and finish approaches to delivering central 'welcome' activities; establishing communities of practice to continually improve academic inductions (the '*University-Wide Transition Network*' and '*Student Peer Support Network*'); developing a toolkit of resources to help Programme Leaders improve their programme inductions; and the development of an online pre-arrival module that all taught students are expected to complete before arriving on campus.

The evolution of the UoS pre-arrival module

The development of pre-arrival resources into a coherent online module for all taught students has been an iterative process over several years. Overall, the project aimed to develop resources aligned to the 'What Works' model for student retention and success, which highlights the importance of 'engagement to promote belonging [which] must begin early and continue across the student life cycle' (Thomas, 2012, p. 16). Central to this model are three spheres: *academic, social* and *services* and our pre-arrival module aims to develop student belonging in each of these domains.

Student partnership has been at the heart of our approach to developing the module. The most obvious partnership activity has been the co-design and co-creation of pre-arrival materials and resources. Not only have students been critical to designing *what* we include, they have also *created* videos, social media, and interactive content that help to ensure that the materials are accessible, engaging and relevant to other students. Students have also added value in the student partnership domain of co-research and co-inquiry (Healey et al., 2014). For example, using web analytics skills developed through their degree studies to research and inquire into usage patterns, contributing to the scholarship of learning and teaching through evaluating student feedback and usage. Table 2.1 shows the development of pre-arrival materials and resources and identifies student partnership activity.

Working effectively with student partners

Student partnership has many positive outcomes; however, it is not without challenges. The following reflections with examples from the project highlight some practical considerations for working effectively with students as partners.

Value student participation

Co-creation inherently recognises that students have valuable perspectives to offer (Cook-Sather et al., 2014). However, there are varying levels of participation from more tokenistic forms of 'consultation' (e.g. rubber-stamping decisions made by staff) through to genuinely student-led initiatives where students 'control decision-making and have substantial influence' (Bovill & Bulley, 2011, p. 5). We employed student partnership at various levels. At the top of the 'ladder of participation' (Bovill & Bulley, 2011), the project employed a student co-lead who had significant influence as a member of the project board and was a workstream lead for developing student communications. Student intern teams working on reviewing and creating resources had control of a prescribed area of the project with some agency in what to include and how to present this. At the other end of the ladder, new students were surveyed and took part in focus groups as part of the ongoing evaluation and iteration of the module.

Practical ways in which student partnership has been valued on the project include:

• Creation of paid internships and roles. Student co-lead and intern roles have represented a significant commitment of time and effort. The creation of paid roles is an important consideration in student partnership work, especially in relation to equality of opportunity. In an economic climate where students increasingly need to take paid work to support their studies, paid internships are more accessible to students who may not be able

Table 2.1 Student Partnership in the Evolution of Pre-Arrival Resources

Development phase	Student partnership activity
Project initiation (2018–19). Development of project aims and objectives. Development of project workstreams. Delivery of 'Welcome' communication plan – schedule of social media posts, videos and tips from key members of staff and students ('Getting to know you') using the #UoSWelcome hashtag.	Recruitment of student co-lead (project board member, co-chair of meetings, workstream lead for development of 'Welcome' communication plan). The student co-lead had strategic influence (in the development of project aims and objectives) as well as being instrumental in delivering the 'Welcome' communications workstream.
Transition to Online Learning (2020–2021). Project aims and objectives revised to support the urgent pivot to online learning during the COVID-19 pandemic. An online pre-arrival module in the VLE designed to support all students with the transition to studying online was developed during Spring 2020. This developed into a pre-arrival transitions module supporting new cohorts enrolling in Sept 2020 and Jan 2021. The module aimed to enhance belonging in an online/ blended learning environment; support the development of practices for studying online; and promote key messages for a safe and secure campus.	Recruitment of 4 project interns (feedback and testing of 'Welcome to Online Learning' module launched Spring 2020). Interns played a critical role in reviewing and co-creating materials for successive iterations of the pre-arrival module in Sept 2020 and Jan 2021. Intern reviews informed several improvements including: • Reducing the amount of content to improve student engagement • Increasing the amount of student co-created content (e.g. advice from current students about studying during the pandemic) • Increasing active learning content (e.g. including interactive polls and quizzes) During this phase, project interns researched and evaluated usage of the pre-arrival module.
Embedding the pre-arrival transition module in business-as-usual (2022-current). Towards the end of the project lifecycle, activity focused on sustaining key elements of transition support in business-as-usual. Maintenance of the pre-arrival module has now moved to business-as-usual within the central Academic Skills Team and this is supported within a workstream of the annual 'Welcome Task and Finish' groups.	Interns applied quantitative and qualitative research skills to evaluate usage, survey and focus group data. Outputs from evaluation work contributed to the overall project evaluation and informed further developments. Interns continued to co-create resources (videos) during this phase as focus shifted to a return to campus-based learning and teaching.

to volunteer their time for free (Evans et al., 2014). Internships also offer enhanced opportunities to develop employability. Practicing applications and interviews, developing professional behaviours and communication skills and offering a space to plan and reflect on development areas can all help students to articulate their employability to future employers (Tomlinson & Anderson, 2021).

- Genuine representation. The creation of a genuine student co-lead role with project board representation was a significant aspect of the project. Project interns were also invited to attend relevant meetings, for example presenting review findings and recommendations directly to the project working group. This direct representation was mutually beneficial for both staff and students. Project interns were initially nervous and excited about presenting to the staff group. The focus of a presentation provided a strong motivation to complete the review task to a high standard. It was important to scaffold and support the interns with this activity, for example by giving them feedback on a 'practice' presentation to help develop confidence. During review at the end of the internship, interns highlighted the presentation as challenging, but rewarding and reflected that this had helped them to develop confidence presenting to senior colleagues.
- Recognition and celebration of success. This could be as simple as providing regular feedback on outputs and developments. We provided regular opportunities to recognise and celebrate success, including positive feedback from senior staff; formal recognition at project boards; and review and celebration of achievements during the closure of the internship. LinkedIn testimonials and letters of recommendation are important forms of recognition that can be transferred to future employment and were highly prized by our project interns.

Build and sustain effective working relationships

Widely cited positive benefits of student partnership include: an 'enhanced relationship of trust', 'increased understanding of the "other's" experience' and 'positively shifted traditional power dynamics between students and academics' (Mercer-Mapstone et al., 2017). Realising these benefits is highly dependent on building and sustaining effective working relationships. The emerging discipline of 'relational pedagogy' offers helpful advice for building relationships in co-creation work and 'showing that we care' and regular, effective communication with students are both critical factors (Bovill, 2020). The emergence of increased virtual and hybrid working post-pandemic challenges the development of effective working relationships (Haas, 2022), but also provides opportunities to make internships more inclusive and accessible, for example to students who have travelled home for the summer and provides interns with valuable experience of working in virtual teams.

The project employed several practical techniques to build and sustain effective relationships with interns, including:

- Induction, icebreakers and team building. We noticed a strong need to develop belonging and identity with our interns that has strong parallels to student induction work. We found that participating in icebreaker activities (for example a group treasure hunt) was an effective way to build effective relationships and social confidence within the intern team. We also found that more structured 'team building' activities were useful in understanding diversity within the team. A 'light-touch' discussion of Belbin questionnaire results (including staff members of the team) was a good way to understand strengths in relation to different team roles and helped to identify gaps (in our case none of the team were 'complete finishers'). Participating as equals with interns in these activities was helpful in terms of disrupting any unhelpful pre-conceptions of how academics and students relate to each other. Developing a clear brief for the task is a critical part of induction. We found that co-creating the brief with interns was an effective way to clarify responsibilities, develop boundaries and identify additional support needed to carry out the brief.

- Effective, regular meetings. Establishing regular (weekly) meetings was a critical factor in developing and sustaining effective relationships, especially during remote working due to COVID-19. Project interns had limited experience of working in virtual teams, and it was important to contract and role-model appropriate behaviours (such as sharing camera and audio in meetings). Being explicit about the opportunity to practice virtual team working and its value as for employability was effective as a motivator for interns to develop their skills. In addition to attending weekly scheduled team meetings, interns were encouraged to meet independently between meetings. This proved to be a valuable form of peer support, especially during periods of social isolation due to the pandemic. Periodic, 1:1 meetings were also important and offered a confidential space for reflection on personal development, exploring any tensions within the group, and identifying individual support needs.

- Providing a space for collaboration. At different times, the project employed interns both on-campus and in virtual, remote working environments. Arranging for an office space for campus-based activity was highly beneficial for building relationships and provided a base for interns to work and socialise. It is critical to provide orientation for interns as part of induction as students may lack confidence accessing 'staff' spaces such as kitchens and common rooms. Virtual working can enable remote students to participate in internships and similar consideration needs to be made for creating a collaborative environment. We found Microsoft Teams to be a suitable environment for hosting virtual meetings, sharing collaborative documents and enabling asynchronous chat between meetings. The use of virtual gestures (such as upvotes and emojis) was also an effective and time-efficient way to sustain relationships, offer positive feedback on developments and build confidence within the team.

Foster mutual benefit through development opportunities

Reciprocity is a critical component of student partnership, and it is essential that all parties 'stand to benefit from' the partnership (Healey et al., 2014). We found it helpful to ask what each of the partners (and most importantly the students!) stood to gain and were intentional about how to realise those benefits (Cook-Sather et al., 2014). Although financial benefit is an important factor that may enable students to engage with paid internships, our experience was that students are most often motivated by the development opportunity (Donald & Ford, 2023).

The following steps were found to be simple, practical ways to enhance the employability benefits for student interns:

- Develop authentic recruitment and selection processes. Recreating the types of recruitment activities used by employers can be highly beneficial in providing students with practical experience of applying for work and is crucial to fair and transparent selection. Systematically offering feedback to applicants ensures that even students who are unsuccessful can gain some benefit from the process.
- Explore motivations and development goals. Explicitly asking about motivations and individual development goals during selection and induction can help to support student development. We asked interns 'why are you applying for this role?' as part of the interview process and 'what do you hope to get from the internship?' during induction.
- Identify development opportunities and challenges. Providing an appropriate amount of challenge in the role and supporting development needs can be effective forms of professional development. Leadership opportunities can be created by assigning leaders for different aspects of the project aligned to individual knowledge, experience, and interests. It is also important to provide relevant training and resources to complete the project tasks (e.g. media production techniques).
- Offer feedback and reflect on development. We provided regular opportunities for staff and peer feedback throughout the internships. Weekly team meetings took the structure of presenting individual progress against objectives, and feedback from all members of the team was encouraged.

Conclusion

Effective transition to studying at university is highly dependent on the development of belonging and student identity, and this can be challenging in an uncertain economic climate with students who have experienced massive disruption to their prior learning.

Online, pre-arrival modules offer accessible opportunities for students to develop belonging early in the 'student lifecycle'. We have found student partnership to be a transformative approach in the development of our online pre-arrival module, and this has fostered collaboration, co-creation and shared decision-making. The insights and perspectives of students have enriched the learning resources, and co-created materials have resulted in a more inclusive and accessible module, with improved engagement and feedback from new students.

Effective practices for student partnership have been critical to achieving successful outcomes. These include valuing student participation, creating and sustaining effective relationships and enhancing the benefits for all partners.

References

Bovill, C. (2020). *Co-creating learning and teaching: Towards relational pedagogy in higher education.* Critical Publishing.

Bovill, C., & Bulley, C. J. (2011). A model of active student participation in curriculum design: Exploring desirability and possibility. In C. Rust (Ed.), *Improving student learning (ISL) 18: Global theories and local practices: Institutional, disciplinary and cultural variations* (pp. 176–188). The Oxford Centre for Staff and Educational Development.

Cook-Sather, A., Bovill, C., & Felten, P. (2014). *Engaging students as partners in learning and teaching: A guide for faculty.* John Wiley & Sons.

Donald, W. E., & Ford, N. (2023). Fostering social mobility and employability: The case for peer learning. *Teaching in Higher Education, 28*(3), 672–678.

Evans, C., Gbadamosi, G., & Richardson, M. (2014). Flexibility, compromise and opportunity: Students' perceptions of balancing part-time work with a full-time business degree. *The International Journal of Management Education, 12*(2), 80–90.

Foster, M. (2011). Engaging students in enhanced academic transitions-a case of online study skills resource SPICE (Student Pre-arrival Induction for Continuing Education). *Journal of Learning Development in Higher Education, 3*, 1–18.

Haas, M. (2022, February 15). 5 challenges of hybrid work – and how to overcome them. *Harvard Business Review.* https://hbr.org/2022/02/5-challenges-of-hybrid-work-and-how-to-overcome-them.

Healey, M., Flint, A., & Harrington, K. (2014). *Engagement through partnership: Students as partners in learning and teaching in higher education.* York: Higher Education Academy.

Hillman, N. (2014). *A guide to the removal of student number controls.* Higher Education Policy Institute.

Mercer-Mapstone, L., Dvorakova, S. L., Matthews, K. E., Abbot, S., Cheng, B., Felten, P., . . . Swaim, K. (2017). A systematic literature review of students as partners in higher education. *International Journal for Students as Partners, 1*, 1–23.

Morgan, M. (2013). Re-framing the 'first year' undergraduate student experience. *The All Ireland Journal of Teaching and Learning in Higher Education, 5*(3), 1441–14418.

Thomas, L. (2012). Building student engagement and belonging in higher education at a time of change. *Paul Hamlyn Foundation, 100*(1–99).

Tilak, J. B., & Kumar, A. G. (2022). Policy changes in global higher education: What lessons do we learn from the COVID-19 pandemic? *Higher Education Policy, 35*(3), 610–628.

Tomlinson, M., & Anderson, V. (2021). Employers and graduates: The mediating role of signals and capitals. *Journal of Higher Education Policy and Management, 43*(4), 384–399.

Woods, K., & Homer, D. (2022). The staff – student co-design of an online resource for pre-arrival arts and humanities students. *Arts and Humanities in Higher Education, 21*(2), 176–197.

3 Traversing obstacles in developing pre-arrival platforms

Kelly Edmunds and Becky Lewis

Our greatest glory is not in never falling, but in rising every time we fall.

—Confucius

As undergraduate students, our impression of our lecturers was one of wisdom, composure and success. Now that we find ourselves in the position of being those 'wise beings', we are less sure of this. Wisdom: yes, composure: mostly, but success: not necessarily, and that is absolutely fine!

Looking at our colleagues within higher education (HE), those who we consider most inspirational are those making the biggest swings: bold changes and radical innovations. However, this bravery is unsustainable without a willingness to risk failure and what is inspirational about these colleagues is how they handle this failure – reflectively, learning from and embracing it as part of the process (Loscalzo, 2014).

We often applaud the successes – the exciting publications and the big grants that are awarded but how often do we applaud all the effort that went into the failures that were experienced along the way? If we sweep failures under the rug, treating them as something to be ashamed of, how can our students learn what an intrinsic part of the process failure is? In this chapter, we reflect on our journey developing pre-university transitions platforms, particularly focusing on our failures: what did not work as well as we had hoped and what we have learnt from these experiences.

When students arrive at university, they tend to be enthusiastic, excited, anxious and overwhelmed. They are typically keen to engage with what the university is offering and want to know what they need to know and what they need to do. They want a roadmap to success. Several years ago, we recognised that our students were changing. Technology was rapidly changing the landscape of teaching and learning within HE, mental health and well-being of society was declining (Carnegie UK, 2021), and consequently, the needs of our students were shifting. Fast forward to today: the needs of our students continue to change but even more rapidly and unpredictably than before.

DOI: 10.4324/9781003427575-5

Historically, the majority of support around the transition into university was through in-person sessions. The sessions were varied – some used Lego and asked students to build something that they associated with a successful student; we had in-person coffee and biscuits with existing students and the more formal welcome lectures from academics. All of these were delivered with great enthusiasm and student feedback was good, if not great, but the pandemic pushed us to change and to innovate as we moved rapidly to a digital platform for our pre-arrival and arrival support. Here, we will evaluate three steps on our journey to optimise our pre-arrival platforms post-pandemic and lay out our plans for the fourth.

Pre-arrival platform version 1; an online 'student zone'

Our first venture into arrival platforms was initiated by our institution early in the COVID-19 pandemic, during the summer of 2020. In response to the rapidly changing and turbulent time, our institution developed a faculty-led online student zone to incorporate pre-arrival and arrival information. This was developed as a page within the virtual learning environment (VLE) (in our case Blackboard) and students were signposted to the site during their registration process. The main drawbacks of this approach were:

i) the site was intended to provide information and signposting to signpost to sources of support rather than academic resources;
ii) the site was developed and maintained by an administrative support team meaning that all changes had to be directed through them;
iii) there was limited functionality for engagement between students and academic staff and
iv) there was very little student input into the content and structure of the platform.

Pre-arrival platform version 2; a Padlet-based transitions toolkit

We wanted to create a resource that new students could engage with as they made their preparations for university; while they were navigating the arrival transition period; and at any subsequent point in their academic journey. We recognised that our own undergraduate experiences do not reflect those of our students and that a resource for our students would be best if informed and developed by students. To ensure that the student voice was central to our pre-arrival resources, we employed three student interns for five weeks. Between them, the students had recent experience of Foundation Year and Level 4 study and represented a range of widening participation groups spanning different ethnicities, genders and age groups.

Their role was to:

i) survey existing students;
ii) to use this to inform the needs of incoming students;
iii) develop the resources which we then built in to our Padlet pages.

This first foray into pre-arrival platforms was with Padlet (see Figure 3.1), a platform that we use in a range of ways in our teaching, making it an obvious choice. The benefits of a Padlet-based resource include:

i) creating Padlet pages does not require a subscription (three Padlets can be created for free);
ii) visitors can access and engage with a Padlet without creating an account;
iii) engagement with a Padlet page can be anonymous;
iv) Padlets can be embedded within a virtual learning environment (VLE) such as Blackboard;
v) engagement can be tracked through likes, comments and posts.

We launched the Padlet-based 'Transitions toolkit' to the incoming 2021 cohort. In total, it comprised 20 resources, all of which had been developed by current undergraduate students (Harrington et al., 2021).

Successes of this platform

The focus on students as informers and creators of the resources in this first iteration of our pre-arrival platform was a real strength. In addition to informing the content of the Padlet, offering a forum for students to share their needs with us empowers and gives them a voice. The unlimited access to the Padlet-hosted resources enabled students to choose which information to access and when, based on their specific needs which should prevent information fatigue. The Padlet platform is free, easy-to-use and requires minimal commitment from the students as they do not need to create an account. We regularly use Padlet as an educational tool, so using it for a pre-arrival platform also helps familiarise students with a tool used within their course.

Drawbacks of this platform

Padlet does not have the capacity for adaptive release of content and so all resources were uploaded in advance, as we did not have capacity to update our platform frequently at the start of the academic year. This meant that our Padlet had all resources available to students immediately. We believed that this would be a strength of the platform, but on reflection, we were concerned that such a library of information at a time of anxiety could result in choice

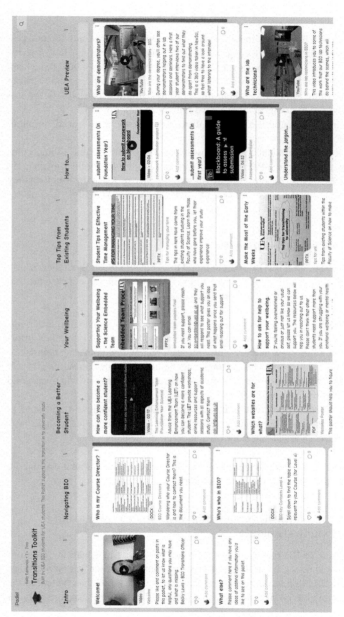

Figure 3.1 Screenshot of the Transitions Toolkit built as a Padlet page to host student-developed resources to support new students from the pre-arrival phase through their undergraduate studies in the School of Biological Sciences at the University of East Anglia.

paralysis with students being unable to engage due to fear of starting in the wrong place. Our Padlet had a non-linear format, with content grouped into themed columns. We believed this format would help students browsing, but in retrospect we think that offering a pathway through the resources would have been beneficial. As with many things, the first step can be the hardest, and showing students where to begin can help them on their journey, particularly for students who might not be aware of what they need support with. We underestimated the amount of information we would need to gather from the platform.

For a more confident audience, who would be comfortable liking, commenting and posting, Padlet would certainly provide useful engagement metrics. However, for our cohort, we had no way of knowing whether they engaged as 'lurkers', were affected by choice paralysis, were limited by accessibility issues or did not engage at all.

Lessons we have learnt from this

Overall, although it was difficult to brand the Transitions Toolkit a success, we were still very proud of the resources developed with our student partners, but we learnt some important lessons from this iteration.

1. Accessibility is key. Students transitioning into university are overwhelmed and worried about doing the wrong thing or missing key information. Offering a pathway through resources will support engagement.
2. It is important to be able to track engagement. Without those metrics, we have no feedback system and no way of students telling us what was good or could be improved.
3. Having student co-creators is incredibly valuable and funding for student interns is generally money well spent. It is easy to underestimate how much has changed since our own undergraduate days.

While we still use Padlet extensively in our teaching, we felt that it was not the right platform for this. We knew that we could do better.

Pre-arrival platform version 3; a VLE-hosted 'preparing for your studies' module

Shifting our Padlet-based pre-arrival toolkit to the virtual learning environment (Blackboard), brought challenges but, more importantly, opportunities. Being mindful that we were moving from a resource which had had all of the content available all of the time, we wanted to bring more structure into our platform.

To coincide with the timescales for student registration and avoid overwhelming incoming students, who may also have had holidays or part-time jobs occupying their time, we decided on a three-week-long module with new content released weekly. The first two weeks of the module were in the pre-arrival phase of student transition to university and the third and final week was arrival week, known as Welcome Week.

All new undergraduate students in the School of Biological Sciences, at both Levels 3 and 4, were automatically enrolled on to the module and had access once they had completed their registration task. Aware that new undergraduate students would not know how to navigate a Blackboard module and thus would not find the pre-arrival resources without signposting, we sent out an email on the Monday of each week to coincide with the release of new content. The email introduced the Blackboard module, provided an access link and outlined the content for that week. In addition to weekly content focused on helping students to prepare for their course and the transition to university life, we also used the module to learn more about our new student cohort (see Table 3.1). The survey included questions about student expectations, well-being, previous education etc. and was available to students throughout the three scheduled weeks of the module (Leggett, 2022). Other than the survey, all module content is available to students for the duration of their studies.

Moving the pre-arrival support to the institution VLE (Blackboard) overcame one of the major weaknesses of the Padlet-hosted previous version. Engagement data from the module show that during the three weeks of the pre-arrival/welcome period, users engaged with module content a total of 969 times (340 incoming undergraduates were enrolled). Engagement with the module extended well beyond the pre-arrival and arrival period. From the launch of the module on 05/09/22 through to 10/02/23, 4822 hits were made on the module. Unexpectedly and to our delight, engagement with the module content continued beyond the first semester with 65 students engaging with the module on 259 occasions during 2023 (to 16/04/23).

Our previous Padlet-based Transitions Toolkit failed to engage students. While we do not have data on passive users (also known as lurkers, (Arnold & Paulus, 2010; Dennen, 2008)), if students had been liking and commenting on posts on the Padlet page, they would have been recorded as active users. Switching to a VLE platform gave us a greater insight into how and when students were engaging with the module content as well as greater control over the adaptive release of content. There are further improvements to be made, but we are now armed with data to help evidence those improvements.

Pre-arrival platform version 4; improving our VLE-hosted preparing for your studies module

Based on our experience, we cannot envisage a better platform for our pre-arrival module than to use the university-supported VLE. As well as helping to familiarise the students with a platform that they will then use for the rest of their studies, it is also a platform that we are familiar with; it provides a wealth of engagement information; has the ability to update and amend

Table 3.1 Outline of the course structure and content for the Preparing for Your Biology Studies pre-arrival module delivered by the School of Biological Sciences at the University of East Anglia in 2022.

Week 1: Preparing for university. Managing expectations, signposting to support. Content released two weeks prior to students arriving on campus.	Informative Resources	– Introduction from the School Senior Advisor – Academic jargon busting. – Time management.
	Activities to engage with	**Journal club**: introduces two research stories from within the department and guide the student to think about the research. This activity was designed to prime students for their first-year Skills module and introduce them to the School community. **Discussion board**: opportunity for students to introduce themselves to the others in their cohort. **Online social**: using course-specific virtual spaces on the virtual meeting platform Wonder and with academic staff present to answer questions and provide conversation starters.
Week 2: Preparing for your studies. Content released one week prior to students arriving on campus.	Informative Resources	– Lab simulations & virtual tour – Lecture advice – Understanding assignments – Writing practice – Using scientific evidence.
	Activities	**Writing concisely**: introduces students to academic writing, with a focus on concise sentences. This activity links closely to content that the students would go on to cover in their first-year Skills module. **Silent sharing**: encourages students to converse with themselves and reflect on how to improve on and develop their critical thinking skills. **Online social**: as in week 1.
Week 3: Welcome week. Content released at the start of student arrival week.	Content Focus	– Exploring the campus – making the most of your lectures – signposting to support and Peer-Assisted Learning.
	Activities	**Nature walk**: engages students with their new campus as well as introducing them to some of the research taking place in the department focusing on the changing sounds of nature. **Unpacking learning outcomes**: provides students with a strategy for decoding learning outcomes and identifying gaps in their understanding and knowledge.
Throughout module		Pre-arrival survey: The questions used within this survey are available via Leggett, 2022.

content smoothly, as well as to release content over time; and includes the functionality to ask students questions so we can learn more about them, their experiences and their needs.

The next version of our pre-arrival offering will be informed by the engagement data of the previous version but also by the knowledge that the needs of our students are changing. The majority of our students have lived their entire lives in a digital world and one that they tend to explore from a relatively narrow viewpoint. Where we can improve on our 2022 module is to make it possible for the students to engage with the content in a more social-media-esque fashion, which is what many of our students are used to. The average undergraduate student has an attention span of 8 seconds (Albright, 2023) and, from regular exposure to social media content, is well-versed in engaging with multiple, short content items in succession, rather than one 20-minute video at a time.

On reflection, the failures to engage students in versions 1 and 2 of our pre-arrival platform were essential to inform version 3 to make it as strong as it was. There is of course still room for improvement, but we have been so pleased with the response from students and have enjoyed the journey.

Our key takeaway lessons from our experiences are that pre-arrival platforms should guide students through the content. Ideally, information should be released gradually and should be bite-sized, relevant, student-informed, accessible and confidence-building.

Acknowledgements

All resources described here were developed in collaboration with University of East Anglia colleagues. The Padlet-based resource was created with Dr Carl Harrington, the subsequent Blackboard module was a team effort with Carl and Dr Helen Leggett, inspired by Helen's experience at Cambridge University. The Blackboard module evolved from a template created by Dr Stephanie Jong.

References

Albright, J. (2023). *Navigating mental health and student engagement.* [Webinar]. Labster, presented February 23, 2023.

Arnold, N., & Paulus, T. (2010). Using a social networking site for experiential learning: Appropriating, lurking, modeling and community building. *The Internet and Higher Education, 13*(4), 188–196.

Carnegie UK. (2021). *Gross domestic wellbeing: 2019/20 GDWe score release.* Retrieved April 26, 2023, from www.carnegieuktrust.org.uk/publications/gross-domestic-wellbeing-gdwe-2019-20-release/

Dennen, V. P. (2008). Pedagogical lurking: Student engagement in non-posting discussion behavior. *Computers in Human Behavior, 24*(4), 1624–1633.

Harrington, C., Howard, J., Hunt, J., Varshani, S., Edmunds, K., & Lewis, R. (2021). Easing transitions to university – a student-led approach. *Zenodo.* https://doi.org/10.5281/zenodo.7853112

Leggett, H. (2022). Pre-arrival survey for the UEA 'Preparing for your biology studies' course. *Zenodo.* https://zenodo.org/record/7779122

Loscalzo, J. (2014). A celebration of failure. *Circulation, 129*(9), 953–955.

Part II

The use of pre-arrival platforms

4 Fostering a sense of belonging

Emma Palmer

Fostering a sense of belonging links with the students' sense of their self-identity and community; all of these can be influenced based on their experience of transition into, and through university. The aim of this chapter is to review challenges that can often impact negatively on the student's sense of belonging, linking with their sense of identity and community, and explore solutions and examples of practice that may be beneficial for university students prior to arriving to university. As a way of analysing, reflecting and considering our practices, the chapter will focus on a fictional case of a student who is starting their degree at a university, with some examples of pre-arrival platforms and practices at the University of Hull that could be a solution. The intended outcome for practitioners is to offer prompts to explore ways of utilising platforms to support students in finding their sense of belonging and community, with some resilience and self-identification, through a transition of change.

Identities, sense of belonging and communities within a period of transition

Pre-arrival and induction can set a good foundation for addressing students' needs and motivations particularly considering identities, belonging and communities, while considering that this is also a critical time of transition. Each of these elements cannot be isolated as they play a significant role together. Should a student have a positive experience of transitioning into and throughout university, they may feel more reassured and confident, and more likely to engage with their peers, thus feeling some connection to their peer group and/or programme.

On the opposite side, transitioning into university can be an isolating experience for students (Fitzgibbon & Prior, 2006) which, if not done well, could have a negative influence on their engagement and motivation, socially and academically (Tinto, 1975). If the transition experience is not meeting the needs of students, this can influence their decision to withdraw from their

DOI: 10.4324/9781003427575-7

studies earlier in their student journey (Jones et al., 2023). It is vital for sectors to consider that transition does not stop as soon as the student starts at university; they will continue to transition in various guises in terms of progression, developmentally and personally. Therefore, there is a need to design transitions to ensure that a range of student needs are met.

The students' evolving identity can be an opportunity for us as academics and practitioners, to develop our practice in supporting all stages of transition: from pre-arrival to graduation. As well as taking into consideration the student perception of identity based on their educational, dispositional, circumstantial and cultural experiences (Thomas & May, 2010), students have intersectional identities and differing experiences that can feed into their own perception of belonging and where they can find this within communities (Palmer, 2020). These perceptions are vitally important for students in their self-development. Morgan (2013) states that universities need to take into consideration multiple identities when designing support and resources which, if utilised effectively, can have a positive impact on the student experience and offer scope for belonging and community in a transition of change.

It is not just at the point of entering university that a sense of belonging is important. Belonging fundamentally can play a role in retention (Thomas, 2012), especially if students can connect to each other and support each other during moments of self-doubt. In this instance, pre-arrival can be a first opportunity to help incoming students find a sense of belonging, which may last well into their future degree years.

Meeting Addie – a fictional student case

Addie (they/them) is a 20-year-old student from the local area, who after failing their AS-Levels three years prior, has been accepted to go onto the BA (Hons) Media Studies with a Foundation Year. They currently live with their partner in a village on the outskirts of the city, where the commute takes up to 1 hour and 20 minutes one way by public transport. They do have a car, though share this with their partner who is working full time so access to this can be restricted. During their AS-Levels, Addie did well on the practical elements but struggled on the written assignments, and at times did not submit. The college did not refer Addie for a dyslexia screener, though there could be indications that they may have a Specific Learning Difference

(SpLD)

They may be deemed as a 'non-traditional' student, though it is important to consider looking beyond such labels and instead identify how their sense of identity may be reflected in their experience of transition into and through university, and how they can find their sense of belonging and community both academically and socially. The use of pre-arrival platforms could potentially help students to not only connect with support and vital information but find their belonging and community at university (Figure 4.1).

Addie's Student Profile

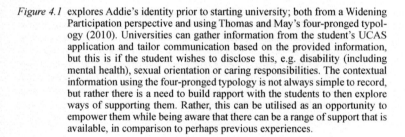

Widening Participation (Office for Students)

- Disability (Mental health and potentially a Specific Learning Difference)

Four-Pronged Typology (Thomas & May, 2010)

Educational
- Completed AS Level but did not progress to A-Level
- Gap between college and university - did full-time work to pay rent
- Struggled with written work, but did well in practical work

Circumstantial
- 20 years old on entry
- Mental Health (anxiety) and potentially Specific Learning Difference (dyslexia)
- Commutes from village 1 hour 20 mins from University
- Lives with partner (not married)

Dispositional
- Non-binary (They/Them)
- Struggles with confidence and self-esteem
- Aspires to work in the media industry

Cultural
- From the local area which is recognised as an area of high income deprivation
- First in the family to go to university

Figure 4.1 explores Addie's identity prior to starting university; both from a Widening Participation perspective and using Thomas and May's four-pronged typology (2010). Universities can gather information from the student's UCAS application and tailor communication based on the provided information, but this is if the student wishes to disclose this, e.g. disability (including mental health), sexual orientation or caring responsibilities. The contextual information using the four-pronged typology is not always simple to record, but rather there is a need to build rapport with the students to then explore ways of supporting them. Rather, this can be utilised as an opportunity to empower them while being aware that there can be a range of support that is available, in comparison to perhaps previous experiences.

Addie's experience of pre-arrival: information overload

Once Addie has received their offer, information is starting to be sent across such as enrolment and some key dates for the academic year, but whilst Addie is looking forward to the next step, there are still some concerns following their previous experience at college. Questions are starting to form for them; A lot of 'What if . . . ?' and 'Can I . . . ?' which starts to worry Addie, but they cannot seem to find a point of contact in the information they are receiving, and they are not sure how to navigate the website.

This can be an overwhelming time for Addie, with several questions and not a lot of answers. There can be a risk of information overload, but there can also be a self-perception for Addie of being judged for asking a potential 'silly question'. Circumstances such as this are not uncommon, as Burke et al. (2016) reported that students' transition into higher education can often be a vulnerable period, and they are likely to have negative feelings about their capability of studying at university. Support is one of the foundations for belonging at university that can help reduce the feeling of 'otherness' and provide well-articulated and clear support (Blake et al., 2022).

To help reduce the possibility of students being overwhelmed with information about support, it can be useful to spread the information out over a time period and offer an opportunity for students to speak to members of staff they will come across within their transition into higher education. There could be scope for interactive pre-arrival platforms to break down the information students receive, but tailor it to their needs too, based on information provided at the time of application e.g. declaration of estrangement from family. Such tailored content may involve key named contacts, with photos accompanying, to provide a face and name to students.

Supporting belonging: An example from University of Hull: MyJourney online modules

All students have access to the University of Hull's MyJourney platform, which provides key information in a series of online modules. At pre-arrival, new students receive a module to read through at key stages prior to arrival: Getting to know Hull (July), Welcome to Hull (August) and Preparing for your Arrival (Early September). Returning students get a dedicated module to avoid repetition of information every year. Each module breaks down key information; from a timeline of what to expect once you have confirmed your offer, engaging with support and systems at the university, and getting to know the School/Department which the programme resides in. Importantly for helping to initiate the sense of belonging, for Foundation Year students, we provide a name and face to the Foundation Year Studies team, with a way of contacting us if students had any questions prior to arriving.

If Addie had access to this pre-arrival platform, this could provide reassurance for them in navigating through the information at key points of their transition, without being overwhelmed and were familiar with support available, both academically and pastorally. Addie is now able to not only receive information needed for the programme but has a named contact to ask key questions and potentially be signposted to additional support. Information being provided in the pre-arrival period is vital for students to help with the transition into university, but commonly students are keen to find connections within their programmes or universities to start establishing friendships and communities.

Addie's experience of pre-arrival: connecting with their community

For Addie, they are keen to see who else is on their programme of study. But they feel very anxious about reaching out to people and would not necessarily know where to start. They are not active on social media, nor would they want to share their personal details so early on. They believe that they will be the oldest student in the room and will be among very young 18-year-olds, so they are unsure how they can connect with their peers.

It is not uncommon for students to explore forums, e.g. The Student Room, or social media to ask for advice from their peers, from making friends to finding information about accommodation prior to arriving at university. This sense of seeking guidance from their peers could be linked with finding a community, particularly a caring place that offers scope for students to connect and support each other academically and, or socially (Boyer, 1990).

Despite 90% of the UK population having social media (Dixon, 2022), there will be a proportion of students who may either refuse to use social media or are not confident in setting up social media platforms. But online spaces can be a way of providing connection to peers and can foster a sense of belonging (Blake et al., 2022). In these cases, platforms that offer an alternative to using social media at pre-arrival stage could be explored to help connect students.

Supporting belonging: The University of Hull's peer support platform

At the University of Hull students could sign up to an app, Umii, prior to arriving at university. The app allows students to connect and match with their peers based on programmes, interests, and societies in a safe and inclusive online environment. This has helped over 1500 students make friends and start fostering a sense of belonging among their peers and the Students' Union Executive Team, who can help answer questions about their student experience before arriving at university. They must confirm their registration to the app with their university email or enrolment details.

For Addie, using a platform designed to interact and connect with others may provide reassurance for them and feel like they are part of a community before starting university, particularly as it could enable students to find others with similar interests and identify ways of being relatable. Apps like Umii can also safeguard and offer students the opportunity to not share personal details unless they build enough of a relationship with their peers. It can also offer scope for students to meet on campus during Induction and be able to navigate the new campus and activities. Over time, concerns such as age differences between 'young' and mature students may reduce as more students are able to relate and build these communities, therefore following the principles of connection as one of the foundations of belonging (Blake et al., 2022).

Conclusion

Throughout Addie's transition into higher education, there are opportunities to identify some of the barriers that Addie may face, with potential solutions. Exploring the use of pre-arrival platforms to connect, and help foster the sense of belonging, could provide institutions with opportunities to design and provide resources to support the transition into university more effectively. But it is important that they recognise the potential challenges students may face too. One example could be digital inequality or skills they may not be confident in using. There could be scope to explore alternatives such as personalised letters/phone calls/text messages, though it can depend on the scalability of the resources available and the student population size.

It may appear challenging for universities to find a good balance of platforms to use; but with the diversity of students in higher education, there is a need to offer inclusive opportunities for them too and utilise pre-arrival platforms that can support the transition into and through university. Hubbard and Gawthorpe (2023) recognise that inclusive universities can, and will, build cultures to help foster belonging and community. Most importantly, it is about connecting with the student to help support their sense of belonging on their journey into their degree. The common theme between the two solutions offered is that there is an empathetic human approach to building a relationship with students like Addie who can find confidence in their new community and feel connected and supported by their university.

Following from this, you may want to consider the following questions when planning pre-arrival activities and communications for belonging:

- What information can be tailored to the student's needs?
- Who can be an identified point of contact for the student, and how can we disseminate the information?
- What platforms can students use to connect with each other?
- What activities and prompts may support students connecting with each other on platforms?
- What are the alternative resources and methods of ways of fostering belonging beyond online platforms?

References

Blake, S., Capper, G., & Jackson, A. (2022). *Building Belonging in Higher Education Recommendations for developing an integrated institutional approach*. WonkHE and Pearson. https://wonkhe.com/wp-content/wonkhe-uploads/2022/10/Building-Belonging-October-2022.pdf

Boyer, E. L. (1990). *In search of community.* ERIC Clearinghouse.

Burke, P., Bennett, A., Burgess, C., Gray, K., & Southgate, E. (2016). *Capability, belonging and equity in higher education: Developing inclusive approaches.* www.newcastle.edu.au/__data/assets/pdf_file/0011/243992/CAPABILITY-ONLINE.pdf

Dixon, S. (2022). *Topic: Social media usage in the UK Statista.* Statista. Retrieved July 20, 2023, from www.statista.com/topics/3236/social-media-usage-in-the-uk/#topicOverview.

Fitzgibbon, K., & Prior, J. (2006). Students' early experiences and university interventions – a time . . . : Ingenta Connect. *Widening Participation and Lifelong Learning, 8*(3), 17–27. www.ingentaconnect.com/content/openu/jwpll/2006/00000008/00000003/art00003

Hubbard, K., & Gawthorpe, P. (2023). *Inclusive higher education framework QAA.* Retrieved July 20, 2023, from www.qaa.ac.uk/docs/qaa/members/inclusive-higher-education-framework.pdf?sfvrsn=209aaa81_6.

Jones, H., Mansi, G., Molesworth, C., Monsey, H., & Orpin, H. (2023). *Transition into higher education* (J. Jarvis & Karen Smith, Eds.). Critical Publishing.

Morgan, M. (2013). *Supporting student diversity in higher education: A practical guide.* Routledge.

Palmer, E. (2020). *Somewhere where they belong: Understanding the impact and influence on UK Undergraduate Students' Transitions, Identities, Sense of Belonging and Communities within a diverse and changing Higher Education Sector* [Dissertation]. University of Hull.

Thomas, L. (2012). *Building student engagement and belonging in Higher Education at a time of change: A summary of findings and recommendations from the What Works? Student retention & success programme summary report.* www.phf.org.uk/wp-content/uploads/2014/10/What-Works-Summary-report.pdf

Thomas, L., & May, H. (2010). *Inclusive learning and teaching in higher education.* https://s3.eu-west-2.amazonaws.com/assets.creode.advancehe-document-manager/documents/hea/private/inclusivelearningandteaching_finalreport_1568036778.pdf

Tinto, V. (1975). Dropout from higher education: A theoretical synthesis of recent research. *Review of Educational Research, 45*(1), 89–125. https://doi.org/10.3102/00346543045001089

5   Using a pre-arrival platform as an induction tool

Fran Garrad-Cole

The main aims of induction to university are to ensure the student has all the information they need for navigating the physical, logistical and educational environment, and to foster a sense of belonging and community through connections to academic or social communities (Thomas, 2012). Research into retention statistics (Turner et al., 2017) suggests that poor support for students transitioning to university can lead to disengagement or withdrawal (Tinto, 1975) and that students are more likely to succeed in their studies if they have developed networks and communities with fellow students (Crosling et al., 2008).

Traditional approaches to higher education induction typically begin and end during Welcome week (see also 'induction week', 'orientation week' and 'freshers' week') when a huge amount of important information and introduction occurs while individuals are also finding new friends, understanding their new environment, and possibly adjusting to being away from home for the first time. Some students may have difficulty registering for their course, or arrive late, and may not receive information about various sessions held during that week. Richardson and Tate (2012) report that students express overload during this intense induction period, leading to boredom and subsequent issues with retention of the information given. The bulk of required information and support services can often be found on an institution's website, but these are unfamiliar platforms and, until the student experiences a difficulty, they may have little motivation for exploring these pages, by which point it may be too late. Students entering higher education, especially those from non-traditional backgrounds (Meuleman et al., 2015), often face additional challenges when acclimatising to university. More recently, those making the transition from school or college to university during, or post, COVID-19 did so following inequalities in access to (and proficiency with) digital technologies and a wide variation in parental support. Together with a lack of social support, this will likely have had a negative effect on their development and mental well-being (Orben et al., 2020) and will have exacerbated the usual transition challenges.

It is important, therefore, to provide appropriate and *timely* information and to appreciate that induction begins long before the student arrives at the

DOI: 10.4324/9781003427575-8

institution and continues beyond the first week. Students begin to form expectations and anxieties and develop misconceptions at various stages towards, and during, their higher education experience (Wilson, 2009), but may hold high levels of excitement and motivation for their upcoming course from the point of accepting their offer (Lee & Dawson, 2011). Early engagement and information sharing can capitalise on this enthusiasm, and a more prolonged approach distributes the induction process in a more manageable fashion. Before arriving at a new institution, the incoming student may not be familiar with higher education terminology (e.g. what is a personal tutor?), institutional structures (colleges, schools, faculties etc.), support systems (where to go for mental health support, money advice) and timetable expectations (utilising private study time, long deadlines for assignments etc.) Increased familiarity, and confidence, with institutional structures and expectations will facilitate engagement and success during induction, which will have a positive effect on motivation and retention.

Pre-arrival induction courses have been used in various programmes including for flexible adult learners via a Massive Open Online Course (MOOC) (Brunton et al., 2018), via co-design with students for arts and humanities courses (Woods & Homer, 2022), and to support the transition for international students (Foster, 2011). However, access to such platforms may not be possible until a student has registered for the course and it may be beneficial to access this information *prior* to choosing a course. Therefore, presenting this 'high-level' basic information in a public, accessible, platform allows the student time to digest and understand essential aspects of induction ahead of the more formal induction week. Extending the induction process, such that it starts at the point of confirmation, recognises the continuous and differing points of transition and provides 'just in time' information and interventions required for student success (Wilson, 2009).

There are several variables that predict first-year student satisfaction, engagement and retention in higher education, which should be considered when designing an induction package. These are summarised in the 'five senses of student success' model (Lizzio, 2011) which considers the 'student lifecycle' towards, into, through and out of higher education on the basis of *purpose, capability, connectedness, resourcefulness* and *culture/identity*. This model has been reviewed, through the lens of post-COVID transition support by Pownall et al. (2022), and in regard to the role of a first-year advisor (Wilson, 2009), and several recommendations and suggestions are made for optimising this approach to induction. The five-sense model of student success has been used in this way by Bangor University as part of a comprehensive induction package, which leads from a pre-arrival platform, through formal induction week and into a year-long self-paced induction programme. The platform (www.bangor.ac.uk/bangor-welcome/be-bangor-ready) enables students to 'Be Bangor Ready' via interactive steps of high-level pre-induction material. This storylined and interactive approach was built by a cross-institutional team from academic schools, service departments and the Students' Union to create an induction journey designed to introduce terms, concepts and activities that will be referred to during welcome week and beyond.

The five senses of student success

Purpose: This represents a student's view of their future careers, their reason for study and their concept of 'making a difference' (Lizzio, 2011). Pownall et al. (2022) suggest that this sense of purpose enables students to seek out appropriate support for both their studies and their personal issues. By including induction activities that require students to clearly articulate their reasons for going to university and help them to systematically develop their strengths and talents, higher education institutions can foster a sense of purpose in new students (Wilson, 2009). Visitors to the 'Be Bangor Ready' site are invited to look ahead to career paths and a short video introducing the *Employability Service* enables students to think about the direction of their studies and their goals for the future before they begin their course – and shows them where to go for help.

Capability: While previous academic ability is an indicator of future success at university, those who have a greater mastery of the academic skills, knowledge and expectations of university will be more 'learning ready' and subsequently more academically successful (Lizzio, 2006, cited in Chester et al., 2013). To support this, Wilson (2009) recommends the development of entry-level academic skills and clear communication of expectations. Pownall et al. (2022) further suggest that working with students as partners to develop and utilise formative (early, low stakes) assessments can help to increase students' confidence with, and understanding of, expectations. In the Bangor model, *Capability* is developed through '*Check your Tech*', which introduces online tools used at Bangor (e.g. Teams and Blackboard), and when and how students will encounter them. This has been particularly beneficial post COVID and addresses some of the inequalities in experience and proficiency with digital skills. The section also reminds of the importance of online enrolment and provides an easy link by which students can do this. Furthermore, '*What to Expect*' is an interactive quiz where students can guess the answer to questions such as 'How long will it take for me to receive feedback on my work?' and are then provided with a short response detailing what can be expected, helping the student to become 'learning ready'.

Connectedness: It is hard for students to develop a sense of belonging in the early weeks of university (Christie et al., 2008), with long-lasting implications for student success and happiness (Wilson, 2009). Students may also experience imposter syndrome and feel as though they have not earned their place or are not suited to university (Pownall et al., 2022). Good working relationships with academic staff (Wilson, 2009) and peer-to-peer support, including joining clubs and societies (Pownall et al., 2022), can help to mitigate these feelings. A sense of community and belonging can be increased through a peer-guide scheme whereby a Year 2 or 3 student is paired with a small group of incoming Year 1 students to act as an informal point of contact and introduce some of the more student-focussed aspects of transitioning to university life. These schemes are hugely successful in supporting students through the less formal, more social aspects, of transition to university (Chester et al., 2013) and the earlier these introductions can take place, even before arrival, the more likely a student is to feel connected to, and part of, their university.

The Bangor platform opens with '*Find your People*' and features a video montage of a range of students explaining what being a Bangor University student means to them, where incoming students can meet people 'like them' and hopefully reduce any feelings of imposter syndrome or of not 'belonging' at university. This section also introduces student vloggers, Facebook communities, and the CampusConnect app where students can join online communities before arrival, and a map depicting all the home locations across the globe of the new Year 1 students. Furthermore, an introduction to the *Students' Union*, free clubs and societies, and moving-in tips for students gives practical advice about how students can find and develop friendships and settle into university life.

Resourcefulness: This relates to a student's ability to navigate the university or institutional systems and be confident (and informed about) seeking appropriate help when needed to manage the balance between study, personal life and paid employment (Wilson, 2009). Pownall et al. (2022) refer to this as the 'hidden curriculum' and note that this will have been particularly exacerbated for students studying pre-tertiary education through COVID. Institutions should avoid assumptions about any prior knowledge students may have about life at university (Pownall et al., 2022) and should provide clear information about who is available to help (and how) and how students may access appropriate support in a timely fashion (Wilson, 2009). The hidden curricula at Bangor is addressed partly through the '*What to Expect*' quiz (see above) but also through '*Know your Campus*' which presents a brief history of the University and its buildings, and interactive maps of both the University's campuses. Later in the platform course '*Access the available support*' provides a short video overview of the student support services available and introduces exactly what a Personal Tutor is. Together these steps provide high-level key support information in a way that is not overwhelming and can be revisited at any point.

Culture/Identity: Chester et al. (2013) describe this as an appreciation of the core values and ethical principles of the institution and in practical terms this can be considered as an understanding of 'how things are done' (Wilson, 2009). The variation in students' prior experiences (especially for those from underrepresented groups and those with disabilities) can lead to inequalities in the feeling of connectedness (Pownall et al., 2022). Conversations with students to discuss and share an understanding of what a university is (Wilson, 2009), and holding those conversations through the lens of equality, diversity and inclusion will help to address systemic inequalities (Pownall et al., 2022). The 'culture' at Bangor University extends from the core values and principles of higher education and includes the bilingual nature of its community. It is important that those who wish to study through the medium of Welsh are aware of opportunities to do so and are informed about the support available. However, it is also important that monolingual students understand the value and importance of the bilingual environment and are clear they do not need to be able to speak Welsh to appreciate the cultural value. A short video in the pre-arrival platform on *the value of bilingualism*, together with an interactive flip-card quiz of basic Welsh words and phrases breaks down the barriers to culture and offers a welcome to all students. In a more general sense, knowing more about 'how things are done' will increase students' confidence with the university culture and this is achieved through short 'a day in the life' videos recorded by current Bangor students.

This pre-arrival platform provides induction starting points which can be picked up individually or by departments after enrolment. These lead into formal induction week activities where students meet their personal tutors, discuss results of a pre-arrival questionnaire (c.f. Smith et al., 2022) in the context of managing expectations, and a host of introductory talks and social activities are made available. However, induction is not complete by the end of that week and Year 1 at Bangor is recognised as an induction year. *'Be Your Best at Bangor'* is a self-directed, non-credit bearing course sitting outside the curricula, which takes first-year students on a journey of learning and adjustment to life at university. Academic, social, financial and developmental support content is released via Blackboard 'just in time' to enable relevant information to be digested and to prevent overwhelm and overload.

Early content focuses on settling in, enrolment and registration, understanding the timetable and getting organised, and on setting achievable goals whereas week four, often a low point for students, encourages students to 'be kind to themselves' through well-being advice. Later in the semester, students are introduced to budgeting, a review of their academic skills with signposting to support, and more detailed explanations about the grading systems and structures ahead of first assignments. Students access a short piece of text or video each week, and then a call to action, in the form of a reflective task, actively engages them in the materials. The material in the year-long induction course is available to personal tutors and can be used to structure and scaffold scheduled tutorial seminars and individual tutee meetings.

Extended transition to higher education is widely recommended and aligning pre-arrival material with an ongoing induction process provides ample opportunity for support, reflection and community building. Pre-arrival platforms are best presented as static, generic, content that is relevant to any incoming student (with links to other, regularly updated, sites for specific information). However, although some content in year-long induction courses may be relevant to all (budgeting, mental health awareness etc.)

content can be tailored to different year groups by registering students on specific year sites.

References

Brunton, J., Brown, M., Costello, E., & Farrell, O. (2018). Head start online: Flexibility, transitions and student success. *Educational Media International, 55*(4), 347–360. https://doi.org/10.1080/09523987.2018.1548783

Chester, A., Burton, L. J., Xenos, S., & Elgar, K. (2013). Peer mentoring: Supporting successful transition for first year undergraduate psychology students. *Australian Journal of Psychology, 65*(1), 30–37.

Christie, H., Tett, L., Cree, V. E., Hounsell, J., & McCune, V. (2008). 'A real rollercoaster of confidence and emotions': Learning to be a university student. *Studies in Higher Education, 33*(5), 567–581. https://doi.org/10.1080/03075070802373040

Crosling, G., Thomas, L., & Heagney, M. (2008). *Improving student retention in higher education: The role of teaching and learning.* Routledge.

Foster, M. (2011). Engaging students in enhanced academic transitions – a case of online study skills resource SPICE (Student Pre-arrival Induction for Continuing Education). *Journal of Learning Development in Higher Education, 3,* 1–18.

Lee, M., & Dawson, G. (2011). *Rethinking student induction.* The Higher Education Academy Subject Centre for Information and Computer Sciences. www.ulster.ac.uk/_data/assets/pdf_file/0003/305436/sddoct15_11.pdf

Lizzio, A. (2011). *The student lifecycle: An integrative framework for guiding practice.* Brisbane. Griffith University. https://studylib.net/doc/6818225/student-lifecycle-framework – docx-103k-

Meuleman, A-M., Garrett, R., Wrench, A., & King, S. (2015). Some people might say I'm thriving but . . . ': Non-traditional students' experiences of university. *International Journal of Inclusive Education, 19*(5), 503–517. https://doi.org/10.1080/13603116.2014.945973

Orben, A., Tomova, L., & Blakemore, S. J. (2020). The effects of social deprivation on adolescent development and mental health. *The Lancet Child & Adolescent Health, 4*(8), 634–640.

Pownall, M., Harris, R., & Blundell-Birtill, P. (2022). Supporting students during the transition to university in COVID-19: Five key considerations and recommendations for educators. *Psychology Learning & Teaching, 21*(1), 3–18. https://doi.org/10.1177/14757257211032486

Richardson, M., & Tate, S. (2012). University is not as easy as A, B, C . . . : How an extended induction can improve the transition to university for new undergraduates. *Emerge, 4,* 11–25.

Smith, S., Priestley, J., Morgan, M., Ettenfield, L., & Pickford, R. (2022). Entry to university at a time of COVID-19: How using a pre-arrival academic questionnaire informed support for new first-year students at Leeds Beckett University. *All Ireland Journal of Teaching and Learning in Higher Education, 14*(2), 1–23.

Thomas, L. (2012). *Building student engagement and belonging in higher education at a time of change: Final report from the 'What Works?'.* Student Retention and Success Programme. Paul Hamlyn Foundation.

Tinto, V. (1975). Dropout from higher education: A theoretical synthesis of recent research. *Review of Educational Research, 45*, 89–125.

Turner, R., Morrison, D., Cotton, D., Child, S., Stevens, S., Nash, P., & Kneale, P. (2017). Easing the transition of first year undergraduates through an immersive induction module. *Teaching in Higher Education, 22*(7), 805–821. https://doi.org/10.1080/13562517.2017.1301906

Wilson, K. (2009, June). The impact of institutional, programmatic and personal interventions on an effective and sustainable first-year student experience. In *12th first year in higher education conference* (Vol. 29). VOCEDplus.

Woods, K., & Homer, D. (2022). The staff – student co-design of an online resource for pre-arrival arts and humanities students. *Arts and Humanities in Higher Education, 21*(2), 176–197. https://doi.org/10.1177/14740222211050572

6   Pre-arrival 'skills' platforms

Bridging the gap between school and university

Laura Boubert and James Fenton

A key predictor of a student's success in transitioning to higher education is the extent and quality of their existing academic skills (Dixon & Beverly, 2015) and their ability to adapt these skills to their new setting (Ashton-Hay & Doncaster, 2021). Although the importance of developing the necessary academic skills is widely recognised, often patchy provision is usually only offered after students have joined their course (Lane et al., 2019) and may be remedial rather than prioritised curriculum content (Davison et al., 2022). In this chapter, we first outline the range of skills that new students transitioning into university are likely to need. The next part explores crucial elements related to how the skills need to be provided, including engagement, motivation and socialization. The remainder of the chapter examines how access to online educational technology can be harnessed to provide incoming university students with pre-arrival skills platforms that enable them to start their courses with enthusiasm and the knowledge they need.

Taxonomy of academic skills

Skills in higher education are commonly divided into hard and soft (or generic) skills (Bennett et al., 1999; Chan et al., 2017; Jääskelä et al., 2018; Widad & Abdellah, 2022). Hard skills can be defined as essential practical skills that can be directly assessed (Emanuel et al., 2021). In contrast, less tangible soft or generic skills include interpersonal skills, decision-making, motivation, self-awareness, effective listening and analytical thinking (Bennett et al., 1999; Emanuel et al., 2021; Jääskelä et al., 2018). A key difference between soft and hard skills is the extent to which they apply to all disciplines and extend beyond university into employment and everyday life.

A further distinction should be made between subject-specific hard skills (e.g. lab techniques, specific software etc.) and more generic transferable academic skills, such as note taking, academic writing, finding and using references, time management and presentation skills (Emanuel et al., 2021). Many academic skills apply across disciplines, so are often called transferable, but they are also an essential tool for supporting the acquisition of the

DOI: 10.4324/9781003427575-9

subject-specific skills which can be demonstrated in summative assessments (Duncan et al., 2008; Kift & Law, 2009; Lane et al., 2019). Importantly, the successful application of skills is underpinned by reflection and critical thinking, key learning outcomes of higher education.

The need for more formal skills development is clearly identified by both academics and students (Jääskelä et al., 2018). Transitioning students report that their academic skills are often insufficient for coping with their first year of higher education (Prowse, 2015; Linceviciute et al., 2021), and this can be further exacerbated by a lack of insight into the skills gap between the expectations of students and lecturers. This gap is often greater for first-generation students who typically have less insight into what to expect at university, with many having expectations of unrealistically high grades (Davison et al., 2022; Elliott et al., 2019). Crucially, many students only become aware of this mismatch after their first assignment (Elliott et al., 2019; Ridge et al., 2021), by which point they might already have become discouraged and disengaged. Simply put, and in line with the Kruger–Dunning effect (Dunning, 2011; Sawler, 2021), some students believe it is going to be easier than it really is, which can lead to them dropping out, failing and developing mental health problems (Davison et al., 2022). A pre-arrival platform could offer an early intervention to help students discover their skills gap, for instance with skills analysis questionnaires, SWOT analyses or problem-based scenarios.

Research has identified that the key areas affected by this lack of student insight that would potentially benefit from early intervention include knowing how to accurately judge the amount of independent study needed and manage time effectively (van der Meer et al., 2010), note taking and utilising academic references (Davison et al., 2022; Elliott et al., 2019), and the requirements (particularly related to writing) of academic submissions (Elliott et al., 2019). Many studies have shown that directed skills support for first-year students in areas such as these can significantly affect both academic and non-academic outcomes.

Evaluations of interventions have found that time management training can improve grades (Wilson et al., 2021) and students reported that it helped them become better at regulating their study time and keeping up with their work (van der Meer et al., 2010). General skills courses have been found to improve self-efficacy and students' outcome expectations (Sheu et al., 2022) while reducing their anxiety about assessments (Wilson et al., 2021). Similarly, academic writing support has been found to rectify the mismatch between students and staff expectations and to increase student confidence and understanding of assessment requirements (Elliott et al., 2019) as well as their expectations and concerns about assessments (Harris-Reeves et al., 2022; Perander et al., 2020). In fact, when Perander et al. (2020) asked students to evaluate their experience of post arrival skills training, most of the negative comments were related to the training coming too late. Crucially, therefore, the benefits of these interventions could be enhanced by bringing them forward to the pre-arrival stage.

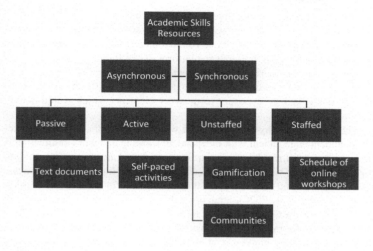

Figure 6.1 The delivery format decision to be made for each element of a pre-arrival academic skills platform.

Essential elements of pre-arrival platforms in addressing skills training needs

All the evidence points towards the potential benefit of pre-arrival skills training for students. The advent of online learning and educational technology provides an ideal opportunity to offer a targeted and rich range of resources that students can access before they have started their studies (Murphy & Tilley, 2019). It is undisputed that learning is enhanced by a student actively engaging with the course content, either in their own time or in live synchronous sessions (Alhazbi & Hasan, 2021; Giesbers et al., 2014; Zeng & Luo, 2023), but the challenge is how to best harness the evolving technology to create resources that are engaging and relevant to each individual student. The key decisions to make in planning such a resource are summarised in Figure 6.1 and include which skills to develop, which platform it should be built on, an existing virtual learning environment (VLE) or a website, whether it should be static and passive or dynamic to support active learning, and the proportion of asynchronous and synchronous content. Ultimately, these factors involve different levels of time, cost and expertise, but the resource can only succeed if it is built on sound pedagogic principles that encourage student engagement (Peters & Romero, 2019).

Motivation, engagement and study self-regulation skills

Universities can provide state of the art resources, but they are only useful if students engage with them. Hardcastle et al. (2019) observed students' willingness to engage with university related issues before arrival, but only on those topics they feel most relevant, such as social integration and housing, which was confirmed by Woods and Homer (2022) when they analysed engagement with their pre-arrival platform. Therefore, it is crucial when designing skill-based resources to create a framework that students will choose to use and engage with (Anthonysamy et al., 2020; Zhu et al., 2016) or they risk a lack of exposure to the very elements which would benefit them most.

This is supported by recent research which suggests that the best predictor of student engagement with independent learning and work completion is their ability to self-regulate their learning, which includes having insight into their strengths and weaknesses (metacognition), good internal motivation and the ability to set and reach realistic studying goals to fulfil the course requirement (Perander et al., 2020). Students lacking self-regulating study skills are typically those most likely to benefit from the training and are also more likely to be extrinsically rather than intrinsically motivated to access the materials in the first place (Anthonysamy et al., 2020). The usual extrinsic motivation of grades or credit is unlikely to apply to a pre-arrival activity, so other incentives will be needed (Bruinsma, 2004) such as rewards or prizes provided in games and apps, or the content needs to be perceived by the student as highly relevant.

Perceived relevance increases engagement, this can be achieved by individualising the content and pace, with staged progression through a variety of interactive skills tasks. Another way to customise content and pace would be to introduce artificial intelligence (Zhang et al., 2021) to provide immediate feedback on students' progress, make ongoing adaptations to their needs and to offer a more bespoke experience (Aljawarneh, 2020) that helps to increase motivation (Vanslambrouck et al., 2018). Many of these tools are currently available, but under-exploited, in commonly used virtual learning environments such as Blackboard or Moodle (Aljawarneh, 2020). The relevance could be further enhanced by involving students in the co-creation of the content, which has also been shown to lead to higher engagement (Davison et al., 2022).

This point was emphasised by Woods and Homer (2022) through their creation and evaluation of a non-compulsory lecturer/student co-created pre-arrival platform for Arts students on Moodle. The module presented and tested students on a range of transition topics, using images, videos, interactive quizzes with links to pre-existing support materials. Findings revealed a high level of uptake by students, and analytics revealed that students engaged most with those topics perceived as most directly related to their own transition. The authors attributed much of the project's success to the co-creation that removed traditional teacher–student hierarchies. The shared approach led to more relevant content, but also a greater degree of social engagement both with the materials and with others on the platform. Their study provides a strong reminder that there is an almost limitless amount of information, both related to academic skills and for pre-arrival more generally, but the real value is likely to lie in a willingness to engage with the materials and then reinforcing it through interaction with others.

Harnessing technology to achieve best practice

It is clear that students want to engage with their peers, as well as with the content of their degrees (Bovill, 2017), and this social engagement leads to many benefits, including increased motivation. Lambert et al. (2014) noted that there are few students of any age who do not utilise social media at some level. Murphy and Tilley (2019) suggest that communities of practice that harness social media can support and reinforce learning while increasing engagement and diminishing alienation (Bovill, 2017). Those communities of practice share similarities with the communities of transitioning students who arrive each year at university, and, in both cases, we see progress from the interaction between participants, whether that be in person or through commonly used social media platforms. The clear recommendation arises that pre-arrival platforms should include and encourage peer-to-peer conversations so that students can create supportive relationships early on as this can lead to them becoming more engaged with how they study by working with peers.

Another increasingly popular approach to enhancing motivation and engagement uses gamification and game-based learning (Wiggins, 2016). Blending principles of online instructional design and gaming, these tools create environments with inbuilt extrinsic motivation (Roohi et al., 2018), providing opportunities for students to interact with others competitively and socially. It also offers the possibility of built in rewards within the game or linked to actual rewards on campus, such as free drinks, stationery or university branded merchandise. This can all provide the extrinsic motivation that we know supports student engagement and motivation. An example of gamification in practice can be seen through work arising from the development of the Westminster Serious Games Platform (wmin-SGP) at the University of Westminster (Economou et al., 2016). Rejecting the static, passive repository model of platform-based skill instruction, the authors designed an online orientation task, the 'Navigating Westminster Game'. The approach meant that the content became self-paced and more authentic with visible, concrete examples provided by the task (Lee, 2018).

Looking ahead

Increasing the ease of access and familiarity with the format will also increase engagement. For example, a dedicated phone application that exploits push technology to invite students to participate in daily tasks and then uses opt-ins to gamification to provide the necessary content (Wiggins, 2016). This can be further added to by including opportunities for students to connect with each other, either through chat functions or extending it to commonly used social media platforms. Such an approach could be supplemented with synchronous content and staffed sessions, where students could work together towards common goals, e.g. creating a presentation (individual or group) on topics related to university orientation. Presentations tap into a range of academic skills (van Ginkel et al., 2015) in addition to providing an opportunity to work with and meet their peers. This type of activity would create a social setting to enhance engagement and reduce the potential alienation linked to online learning (Bovill, 2017). Crucially, practicing skills with their peers can address students' known concerns about socialising in a new context and public speaking (Grieve et al., 2021) while providing exposure and practice for transferable oral skills (de Grez et al., 2014; Dixon & Beverly, 2015) that can be shared and developed as they join their degrees.

Conclusion

The role and perceptions of academic skills have changed over time, with a shift in emphasis towards areas such as employability and other post-degree skills for life beyond university (Dixon & Beverly, 2015), alongside a more inclusive recognition of students' diverse needs (Burt, 2015). More broadly, we can see a move beyond the existing remediation and deficit models (Hutchinson & Waters, 1987) towards more constructive pre-arrival skills support enabling and supporting students as they begin their degrees. Better ways to harness pre-arrival platforms to effectively deliver academic skills are emerging; however, few so far offer the fully anticipated ubiquitous learning environment, and it is essential that future pre-arrival platforms are thoroughly evaluated to ensure that they are meeting the needs of new students (Lane et al., 2019).

Whatever options are chosen, such platforms need to be an effective part of an ongoing programme that recognises individual needs to motivate student engagement to develop their self-regulation skills. Socialization beyond online interaction has been identified as a key way of enabling that. Utilised effectively, skills training via pre-arrival platforms can become a way of addressing higher education's equality and diversity aspirations, plugging acknowledged gaps, and levelling the playing field so that a greater number of students can succeed (Davison et al., 2022) as they enter university and successfully negotiate their degrees.

References

Alhazbi, S., & Hasan, M. A. (2021). The role of self-regulation in remote emergency learning: Comparing synchronous and asynchronous online learning. *Sustainability (Switzerland)*, *13*(19), 1–12. https://doi.org/10.3390/su131911070

Aljawarneh, S. A. (2020). Reviewing and exploring innovative ubiquitous learning tools in higher education. *Journal of Computing in Higher Education*, *32*(1), 57–73. https://doi.org/10.1007/s12528-019-09207-0

Anthonysamy, L., Koo, A. C., & Hew, S. H. (2020). Self-regulated learning strategies and non-academic outcomes in higher education blended learning environments: A one decade review. *Education and Information Technologies*, *25*(5), 3677–3704. https://doi.org/10.1007/s10639-020-10134-2

Ashton-Hay, S., & Doncaster, N. (2021). Student success and retention: What's academic skills got to do with it? *Journal of Academic Language & Learning*, *15*(1), 102–116.

Bennett, N., Dunne, E., & Carré, C. (1999). Patterns of core and generic skill provision in higher education. *Higher Education*, *37*(1), 71–93. https://doi.org/10.1023/A:1003451727126

Bovill, C. (2017). Maintaining criticality: Attempts to stop an unacceptable proportion of students from feeling alienated. *The Journal of Educational Innovation, Partnership and Change*, *3*(1), 14. https://doi.org/10.21100/jeipc.v3i1.681

Bruinsma, M. (2004). Motivation, cognitive processing and achievement in higher education. *Learning and Instruction*, *14*(6), 549–568. https://doi.org/10.1016/j.learninstruc.2004.09.001

Burt, B. A. (2015). Student engagement in higher education: Theoretical perspectives and practical approaches for diverse populations (2nd edition) ed. by Stephen John Quaye and Shaun R. Harper. *Journal of College Student Development*, *56*(3), 311–313. https://doi.org/10.1353/csd.2015.0026

Chan, C. K. Y., Fong, E. T. Y., Luk, L. Y. Y., & Ho, R. (2017, August). A review of literature on challenges in the development and implementation of generic competencies in higher education curriculum. *International Journal of Educational Development*, *57*, 1–10. https://doi.org/10.1016/j.ijedudev.2017.08.010

Davison, E., Sanderson, R., Hobson, T., & Hopkins, J. (2022). Skills for success? Supporting transition into higher education for students from diverse backgrounds. *Widening Participation and Lifelong Learning*, *24*(1), 165–186. https://doi.org/10.5456/wpll.24.1.165

de Grez, L., Valcke, M., & Roozen, I. (2014). The differential impact of observational learning and practice-based learning on the development of oral presentation skills in higher education. *Higher Education Research and Development*, *33*(2), 256–271. https://doi.org/10.1080/07294360.2013.832155

Dixon, G., & Beverly, G. T. (2015). Improving undergrad presentation skills. *ASEE Annual Conference and Exposition, Conference Proceedings*, *122nd ASEE* (122nd ASEE Annual Conference and Exposition: Making Value for Society). https://doi.org/10.18260/p.24270

Duncan, M., Quinn, C., & Creagh, T. (2008). *Operationalising first year curriculum principles* (pp. 1–5). First Year Experience Director, Queensland University of Technology.

Dunning, D. (2011). The Dunning-Kruger effect. On being ignorant of one's own ignorance. In *Advances in experimental social psychology* (1st ed., Vol. 44). Elsevier Inc. https://doi.org/10.1016/B978-0-12-385522-0.00005-6

Economou, D., Doumanis, I., Pedersen, F., Kathrani, P., Mentzelopoulos, M., Bouki, V., & Georgalas, N. (2016). Westminster Serious Games Platform (wmin-SGP) a tool for real-time authoring of roleplay simulations for learning. *EAI Endorsed Transactions on Future Intelligent Educational Environments*, 2(6), 151524. https://doi.org/10.4108/eai.27-6-2016.151524

Elliott, S., Hendry, H., Ayres, C., Blackman, K., Browning, F., Colebrook, D., Cook, C., Coy, N., Hughes, J., Lilley, N., Newboult, D., Uche, O., Rickell, A., Rura, G. P., Wilson, H., & White, P. (2019). 'On the outside I'm smiling but inside I'm crying': Communication successes and challenges for undergraduate academic writing. *Journal of Further and Higher Education*, 43(9), 1163–1180. https://doi.org/10.1080/0309877X.2018.1455077

Emanuel, F., Ricchiardi, P., Sanseverino, D., & Ghislieri, C. (2021, December). Make soft skills stronger? An online enhancement platform for higher education. *International Journal of Educational Research Open*, 2, 100096. https://doi.org/10.1016/j.ijedro.2021.100096

Giesbers, B., Rienties, B., Tempelaar, D., & Gijselaers, W. (2014). A dynamic analysis of the interplay between asynchronous and synchronous communication in online learning: The impact of motivation. *Journal of Computer Assisted Learning*, 30(1), 30–50. https://doi.org/10.1111/jcal.12020

Grieve, R., Woodley, J., Hunt, S. E., & McKay, A. (2021). Student fears of oral presentations and public speaking in higher education: A qualitative survey. *Journal of Further and Higher Education*, 45(9), 1281–1293. https://doi.org/10.1080/0309877X.2021.1948509

Hardcastle, K., Cook, P., & Sutherland, M. (2019). Improving student transition and retention; a netnographic insight into information exchange and conversation topics for pre-arrival students. *Journal of Perspectives in Applied Academic Practice*, 7(1), 47–56.

Harris-Reeves, B., Pearson, A., & Massa, H. (2022). Exploring the expectations and experiences of first year students undergoing a tailored transition initiative. *Journal of University Teaching and Learning Practice*, 19(3). https://doi.org/10.53761/1.19.3.16

Hutchinson, T., & Waters, A. (1987). *English for specific purposes*. Cambridge University Press.

Jääskelä, P., Nykänen, S., & Tynjälä, P. (2018). Models for the development of generic skills in Finnish higher education. *Journal of Further and Higher Education*, 42(1), 130–142. https://doi.org/10.1080/03098 77X.2016.1206858

Kift, S., & Law, F. (2009, July). Intentional first year curriculum design as a means of facilitating student engagement: Some exemplars. *12th Pacific Rim First Year in Higher Education Conference*, 1–10.

Lambert, C., Erickson, L., Alhramelah, A., Rhoton, D., Lindbeck, R., & Sammons, D. (2014). Technology and adult students in higher education: A review of the literature. *Issues and Trends in Educational Technology*, *2*(1), 1–19.

Lane, M., Moore, A., Hooper, L., Menzies, V., Cooper, B., Shaw, N., & Rueckert, C. (2019). Dimensions of student success: A framework for defining and evaluating support for learning in higher education. *Higher Education Research and Development*, *38*(5), 954–968. https://doi.org/10.1080/0729 4360.2019.1615418

Lee, K. (2018). Everyone already has their community beyond the screen: Reconceptualizing online learning and expanding boundaries. *Educational Technology Research and Development*, *66*(5), 1255–1268. https://doi. org/10.1007/s11423-018-9613-y

Linceviciute, S., Ridge, Damien T., Smyth, N., Cartwright, T., Sebah, I., Bryant, K. and Woolston, J. (2021). *Added Value Report: University of Westminster Transformation in Students Project*. London University of Westminster. https://doi.org/10.34737/v4qqx

MacFarlane, K. (2018). Higher education learner identity for successful student transitions. *Higher Education Research & Development*, *37*(6), 1201–1215.

Murphy, H., & Tilley, E. (2019). Libraries supporting transition: Developing a pre-arrival Open Educational Resource (OER) for taught master's students. *New Review of Academic Librarianship*, *25*(2–4), 271–294. https://doi.org/ 10.1080/13614533.2019.1622580

Perander, K., Londen, M., & Holm, G. (2020). Supporting students' transition to higher education. *Journal of Applied Research in Higher Education*, *13*(2), 622–632. https://doi.org/10.1108/JARHE-01-2020-0005

Peters, M., & Romero, M. (2019). Lifelong learning ecologies in online higher education: Students' engagement in the continuum between formal and informal learning. *British Journal of Educational Technology*, *50*(4), 1729–1743. https://doi.org/10.1111/bjet.12803

Prowse, A. (2015). *Student induction and transition: Reciprocal journeys*. Subscriber Research Series, 2015–2016. www.qaa.ac.uk/en/Publications/ Documents/Subscriber-Research-Reciprocal-Journeys.pdf

Roohi, S., Takatalo, J., Guckelsberger, C., & Hämäläinen, P. (2018, April). Review of intrinsic motivation in simulation-based game testing. *Conference on Human Factors in Computing Systems – Proceedings*, 1–13. https://doi.org/10.1145/3173574.3173921

Sawler, J. (2021). Economics 101-ism and the Dunning-Kruger effect: Reducing overconfidence among introductory macroeconomics students. *International Review of Economics Education*, *36*(February 2020), 100208. https://doi.org/10.1016/j.iree.2020.100208

Sheu, H-B., Chong, S. S., & Dawes, M. E. (2022). The chicken or the egg? Testing temporal relations between academic support, self-efficacy, outcome expectations, and goal progress among college students. *Journal of Counseling Psychology, 69*(5), 589–601. https://doi.org/10.1037/cou0000628

van der Meer, J., Jansen, E., & Torenbeek, M. (2010). "It's almost a mindset that teachers need to change": First-year students' need to be inducted into time management. *Studies in Higher Education, 35*(7), 777–791. https://doi.org/10.1080/03075070903383211

van Ginkel, S., Gulikers, J., Biemans, H., & Mulder, M. (2015). Towards a set of design principles for developing oral presentation competence: A synthesis of research in higher education. *Educational Research Review, 14*, 62–80. https://doi.org/10.1016/j.edurev.2015.02.002

Vanslambrouck, S., Zhu, C., Lombaerts, K., Philipsen, B., & Tondeur, J. (2018). Students' motivation and subjective task value of participating in online and blended learning environments. *Internet and Higher Education, 36*(September 2017), 33–40. https://doi.org/10.1016/j.iheduc.2017.09.002

Widad, A., & Abdellah, G. (2022, February). Strategies used to teach soft skills in undergraduate nursing education: A scoping review. *Journal of Professional Nursing, 42*, 209–218. https://doi.org/10.1016/j.profnurs.2022.07.010

Wiggins, B. E. (2016). An overview and study on the use of games, simulations, and gamification in higher education. *International Journal of Game-Based Learning, 6*(1), 18–29. https://doi.org/10.4018/IJGBL.2016010102

Wilson, R., Joiner, K., & Abbasi, A. (2021). Improving students' performance with time management skills. *Journal of University Teaching and Learning Practice, 18*(4). https://doi.org/10.53761/1.18.4.16

Woods, K., & Homer, D. (2022). The staff – student co-design of an online resource for pre-arrival arts and humanities students. *Arts and Humanities in Higher Education, 21*(2), 176–197. https://doi.org/10.1177/14740222211050572

Zeng, H., & Luo, J. (2023). Effectiveness of synchronous and asynchronous online learning: A meta-analysis. *Interactive Learning Environments*, 1–17. https://doi.org/10.1080/10494820.2023.2197953

Zhang, Y., Qin, G., Cheng, L., Marimuthu, K., & Kumar, B. S. (2021). Interactive smart educational system using AI for students in the higher education platform. *Journal of Multiple-Valued Logic and Soft Computing, 36*(1), 83–98.

Zhu, Y., Au, W., & Yates, G. (2016). University students' self-control and self-regulated learning in a blended course. *Internet and Higher Education, 30*, 54–62. https://doi.org/10.1016/j.iheduc.2016.04.001

7   How can pre-arrival platforms prepare students to engage with careers offerings through their degree?

Victoria Wilson-Crane

There is an expectation that universities registered with the Office for Students deliver outcomes recognised and valued by employers. This chapter presents a case study to demonstrate how a provider of education in the UK provides opportunities for international students to gain employability knowledge, skills and experience throughout programmes. Prior to formal learning commences, this is achieved via an online offer called Pathways Preview.

The pathway to employability

Building good habits from an early stage means students better recognise the wealth of learning opportunities on offer at university. Exposure to the kinds of formal and informal learning students will encounter at university, before they arrive, means students can benefit from the chance to try different activities in a low-stakes, supportive environment, where their individual needs can be taken into consideration. Students can begin to work towards skill recognition programmes, even without realising it, which could give them some confidence on progression, when they notice they are at an advantage, compared to other students.

From our own research with the Higher Education Policy Institute (HEPI), this learning is important to students and is not an add-on; it is expected although such expectations are not always met:

> *An overwhelming majority of international students say the careers support (82%) and employability skills (92%) they thought they would receive, were 'important' or 'very important' when choosing their university. Yet only around half (52%) think their institution in the UK is doing well at satisfying the careers support needs of international students.*
>
> (Higher Education Policy Institute & Kaplan International Pathways, 2021).

DOI: 10.4324/9781003427575-10

A similar experience is reported by Nachatar Singh (2023) following their small-scale study involving students at one Australian university, finding that support was focused primarily on meeting the needs of domestic students (2023, p. 7). Interesting, given the financial investment international students, particularly, make into their futures and, in turn, the financial gains of the higher education institutions (HEIs).

The initial impact of the COVID-19 pandemic accelerated the work towards devising a pre-arrival offer for students. In considering the various options we had for an online learning offer, we agreed that orienting students towards employability skills was one potential way to get students engaged and, in turn, could lead to better retention.

The Kaplan International Pathways case study

Each year, Kaplan International Pathways prepares more than seven thousand international students from over 100 different countries and regions, for degree-level study in the UK. The majority of students are studying pathways programmes, face-to-face, at ten colleges in England and Scotland, as well as a growing number of students joining remotely from their home countries on discrete digital-only offerings.

Pathways programmes bridge gaps in knowledge from prior learning experiences and, crucially, help students develop academic and personal skills vital for success in higher education. Some students also require English Language training to achieve the language entry requirement for their chosen degree programmes. Language tuition for those students is integral to the course and tailored to meet the individual students' needs.

Pathways programmes are short and intensive, with duration normally predicated upon the language ability of students on entry. Students hold qualifications that do not permit entry to the universities directly. Foundation Certificate programmes qualify students to join the Frameworks for Higher Education Qualifications of UK Degree-Awarding Bodies (FHEQ) Level 4. International Year One programmes are for students destined for Level 5 FHEQ provision. Graduates who need to develop academic skills and language ability in order to study at postgraduate level at UK universities take pre-masters programmes. Successful completion of pathways courses opens up access to thousands of degrees for students who would, otherwise, have this opportunity denied.

Pathways preview

Pathways Preview is an early, introductory instance of the virtual learning environment which enables students to engage with Kaplan and their college in the immediate weeks before, to the start of their programme. Offering such a resource was something that had been considered prior to 2020 but work was accelerated given the pressing need in the extremely unusual circumstances of the COVID-19 pandemic.

Pathways Preview offers a light introduction to some of the important key transferable and communication skills students need in the workplace, to help them navigate their pathways, university courses *and* their future careers. The focus was not only upon developing these skills but also highlighting the other features of our student experience, which prospective students may not be expecting. Taking initial inspiration from The Future of Jobs Report (World Economic Forum, 2016) as well as emphasis on abilities and basic skills such as ICT Literacy, the pre-arrival activities have a focus on development of cross-functional skills such as coordinating with others, emotional intelligence and people management (p29), as these are vital for success both at university and beyond. For example, collaborative learning is a key feature, given we know how much students can find this challenging at university and it is such an important skill for future success in working life. Students are introduced to activities in Pathways Preview, and during Welcome Week to collaborate with one another and to communicate effectively with students who are from different cultural, religious and linguistic backgrounds.

Design and development of pathways preview

Montgomery's work on the social capital of international students indicates that students may need particular support to make connections with other students. Without this, educational and personal attainment may be affected (Montgomery, 2010, p. 70). Ways to develop these skills are embedded in the pathways journey. For example, one specific and very deliberate way this is achieved is via Life and Career Skills activities which take place between each five-week learning cycle. Students told us they wanted the chance to meet students from different courses, and who were studying at different levels, to help expand their networks. During these weeks, students work on interdisciplinary topics such as *The World of Work and Enterprise* and *Celebrating Diversity* and awareness is raised of other opportunities for students to continue to learn, with the aim that they will be prepared to engage optimally with careers offerings once enrolled on their degree programmes.

Even if engagement is passive, cursory or instrumental during the pre-degree period, the consistency and regularity of the message helps students to recognise the value. Elements of the Employability Framework are branded as Career Focus which guides students and makes overt the connection between different activities and interventions. The work of Briggs *et al* (2012) advises that one of the things 'potential students benefit from' is 'activities that enable learning *about* higher education'. (p18) This implies imparting *knowledge* but from our experience, there is value in helping students start on their journey of developing the necessary *skills* to be able to thrive at university. Hodgkin and Packer mention 'the ability to develop . . . clear ideas around career goals are key in supporting a smooth transition to university' (2023, p. 5). Picton et al. (2018) tell us

> *belonging can also influence success through its impact on engagement. For example, that sense of alienation may create anxiety, which then inhibits participation in classroom discussions hampering both behavioural and emotional engagement. Belonging can also have a positive impact on well-being.*
>
> (p10).

Conrad's research (2002) observed that learners' engagement with online courses depended on the learning materials and less so on instructors; however, this would have been in a time before synchronous participation was expected and normalised. Work with our students indicates that they value time spent getting to know teachers and their classmates through deliberate, planned activities and resources on the pre-arrival platform, which, in turn, helped with future engagement. Pownall et al. (2021) concur. They mention Lizzio's (2006) 'five senses of success' for successful transition to university:

- Sense of capability
- Sense of connectedness
- Sense of purpose
- Sense of resourcefulness
- Sense of academic culture

Building relationships with peers and staff, identifying with the university and appreciating the values and principles of higher education (2021, p. 5) seemed particularly pertinent to students in transition from home contexts to quite different living and learning environments. The Pathways Preview section on Social and Academic Engagement has advice to help students remain connected with their college and classmates to meet this need.

The QAA (2022) has tried to address the hidden curriculum which, for some international students, has additional cultural dimensions given students most likely need to make significant adjustments from their previous learning experiences to pathways, and then on to university and the workplace. Particular focus on terminology has been helpful as this can be challenging for non-native speakers. One aim of the pre-arrival package on assessment, for example, is to help students understand some of the common types of assessment they will encounter later in their course and to help them understand the phrases we commonly use in assessments both at pathways and in universities in the UK.

Against this background, only around half of students think that their university is providing careers support to meet their needs. Pathways Preview aims to set the scene early in the programme to show students the relevance of the skills they will develop, to both the imminent degree-level study and to the transition to working life beyond university. For example, one of the learning packages helps students to develop networking skills and introduces the various professional networks a student will be supported to join, while on their programme.

While the provision of Pathways Preview had its genesis as a COVID-19 response, it has become an opportunity to further our personalised learning approach with students. There is now confidence that students have both the equipment and the technical skills to be able to engage meaningfully, online, prior to their pathways programmes commencing. All of this work has enabled us to embed the skills development and employability offer, from before day one, of pathways courses. This has helped those students who are less aware of the priority and placement of this strand of their learning, to find out more and even start work on this, from very early in their higher education experience.

The impact of pathways preview

So has Pathways Preview been a success? In the initial few months, there were several thousand page views growing steadily to nearly 115,000 page views across intakes between May 2020 and August 2022. As measured in numbers of page hits, we would say yes, with page view monitoring indicating an average of several unique page views per student.

In the end-of-programme Student Experience Surveys in 2021 and 2022, students commented that they were helped to understand and learn to adapt to the differences between their home cultures and that of the UK. Students said they learned new skills they would not have previously thought about as important, and their confidence had improved. Most importantly, for the purposes of this chapter, 91% of students in Summer 2022 agreed that their programme helped them develop useful employability skills (n=2360).

Pathways Preview has become a permanent feature of the pathways offering at Kaplan International. We will seek to continue to grow this, with student input, in order to develop vital knowledge and employability skills against a backdrop of rapidly changing needs and expectations of students and employers in the world of work of the future.

References

Briggs, A. R., Clark, J., & Hall, I. (2012). Building bridges: Understanding student transition to university. *Quality in Higher Education, 18*(1), 3–21.
Conrad, D. L. (2002). Engagement, excitement, anxiety, and fear: Learners' experiences of starting an online course. *The American Journal of Distance Education, 16*(4), 205–226.

Higher Education Policy Institute and Kaplan International Pathways (2021). *International students need more relevant careers support if UK is to remain a destination of choice.* Accessed from: https://www.hepi. ac.uk/2021/10/14/international-students-need-more-relevant-careers-support-if-uk-is-to-remain-a-destination-of-choice/

Hodgkin, K., & Packer, R. (2023). 'I feel like i identify as a university student, I just don't identify with my university'–how first-year students developed their identities during the COVID-19 pandemic. *International Journal of Educational and Life Transitions, 2*(1), 1–13, Article 10.

Lizzio, A. (2006). *Designing an orientation and transition strategy for commencing students. A conceptual summary of research and practice.* First Year Experience Project. Griffith University.

Montgomery, C. (2010). *Understanding the international student experience.* Palgrave Macmillan.

Nachatar Singh, J. K. (2023). Unequal opportunities in accessing employability-related programmes: South Asian graduates' experiences in Australia. *Higher Education Quarterly, 00*, 1– 14.

Picton, C., Kahu, E. R., & Nelson, K. (2018). 'Hardworking, determined and happy': First-year students' understanding and experience of success. *Higher Education Research & Development, 37*(6), 1260–1273. https://doi. org/10.1080/07294360.2018.1478803 (pp. 9–17)

Pownall, M., Harris, R., & Blundell-Birtill, P. (2021). Supporting students during the transition to university in COVID-19: Five Key considerations and recommendations for educators. *Psychology Learning & Teaching, 21*(1), 3–18.

Quality Assurance Agency. (2022). *Unpacking your hidden curriculum: A guide for educators.* QAA.

World Economic Forum. (2016). *The future of jobs report.* World Economic Forum.

Part III

Diversity in pre-arrival platforms

8 Creating a pre-arrival platform that supports international student transition into UK higher education

Sarah Watson and Hengyi Wang

Data from the Higher Education Statistics Agency (HESA) presents a 10.2% awarding gap in 2020/21 between UK-domiciled and China-domiciled students in UK higher education institutions (HEIs), with the gap reaching as high as 44.0% in some institutions. To help close this awarding gap, it is crucial to understand the China-domiciled student transition experience in UK HEIs and respond to the specific needs that arise (Smith, 2020). Unfortunately, this type of responsiveness rarely happens in a sector that still primarily caters for UK-domiciled, white, middle-class students (Edwards, 1993; Cotton et al., 2016).

Aiming to improve the experiences of China-domiciled students, and help close the awarding gap, this research project interviewed 13 students from mainland China in their home language (Mandarin). The interviews focused on their transition experiences into year two of an undergraduate business degree, having directly entered university from a UK-based, international year one course (IYO) at a partner institution. The qualitative results then helped the researchers co-create, with two students of Chinese heritage, an intercultural welcome pack to aid transition during pre-arrival and while at university.

The challenges of transition for international students

International students' transitions into UK Higher Education are often fraught with challenges (Dooey, 2010; Menzies & Baron, 2014). These have been related to language skills (Berman & Cheng, 2001; Sherry et al., 2010; Halic et al., 2009), comprehending and applying new ways of learning, and adjusting to new social and cultural environments (Debray & Spencer-Oatey, 2019; Sovic, 2012; Tian & Lowe, 2014; Sherry et al., 2010). Well-being issues related to this acculturation, such as stress, isolation and homesickness, have also been identified (Yakunina et al., 2013; Sawir et al., 2008; Hendrickson et al., 2011). Specific emphasis has been placed on language barriers and learning barriers (such as encountering new academic concepts

DOI: 10.4324/9781003427575-12

and pedagogical practices) in the international student experience (Ryan & Viete, 2009), particularly in the context of China-domiciled student transition (Willis & Sedghi, 2014). Ryan and Viete (2009) relate these barriers to lack of intercultural provision within institutions.

One of the ways that international student transition can be supported is when the host provides opportunities for intercultural bridging, whereby students maintain ties to their home cultures as they are introduced to life in UK HEIs (Moores & Popadiuk, 2011). The need for intercultural bridging places demands on institutions for more inclusive transition support that commits to reciprocal adaptation (Volet & Ang, 2012), whereby institutions value the rich and diverse pre-entry experience of international students (Dippold et al., 2022; Ryan, 2011; Tran, 2020).

Institutions can provide a form of intercultural bridging through undertaking co-creation with their international students. Co-creation is particularly important for students and staff of colour because traditionally the university has not been designed for these non-normative groups. The institution can, therefore, often feel monocultural and exclusionary (Fraser & Usman, 2021).

The aim of this research was to develop a tailored transition support bilingual welcome pack for China-domiciled students about to begin studying at a UK HEI. The research was underpinned by two questions:

1. How do China-domiciled students perceive their transition experience?
2. Drawing on these experiences, how can UK HEIs provide tailored prearrival transition support for their China-domiciled students?

Step 1: The interviews

Interviewees were students from mainland China, who directly entered year two of their business degree programme, having studied an IYO course. Before interviews were undertaken, ethical approval (ER/SW657/1) was secured. To get honest and candid responses from students, qualitative interviews were carried out in the student's home language. Conducting the interviews in Mandarin allowed students to articulate themselves in a comprehensive way. This approach also underpinned the ethos of the project, which looked to expound the notion that students should utilise their 'home culture and language as part of the learning process' (Jabbar & Mirza, 2019, p. 8). The interviews were transcribed from Mandarin to English by the project's interviewer and co-lead researcher.

Interviews explored academic and personal experiences of transitioning to university in year two. These gave insight into what works in the current transition process and highlighted further support needed. The information generated by the interviews helped generate a welcome pack, which was co-created with two university students from Chinese backgrounds. This type of co-creation not only advocated students-as-creators (Cook-Sather et al., 2014), but also encouraged students to bring their cultural backgrounds into the institution (Ryan, 2011).

Step 2: Analysing the findings

The findings are structured around the first three cognitive dimensions of Bloom's taxonomy (Krathwohl, 2002), starting with the most basic dimension of learning: remembering. Moving on from remembering, the dimensions of learning become increasingly more skilled as we move to the understanding and application levels.

Independent learning

After studying for the IYO course, interviewees knew independent learning was important, but many also indicated their struggles to truly understand what it was and apply it. Figure 8.1 illustrates the potential barriers international students experience when undertaking independent learning, which can stop the student progressing from the most basic dimension of learning to the more complex. The arrows indicate a route of successful independent learning, moving from remembering to application.

At the remembering level, more than half of the interviewees recognised that greater independent learning is required at university compared to their previous educational experience in IYO. Although most students know that

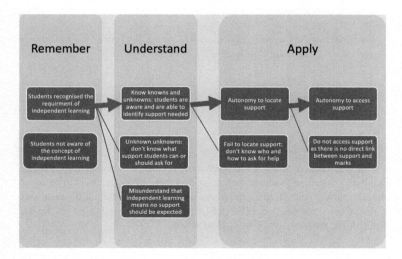

Figure 8.1 Cognitive dimensions of independent learning

they are expected to learn independently, they do not always understand what this means.

At the understanding level, students do not always comprehend that independent learners can still seek support when needed (Kohan et al., 2017). The misunderstanding of what independent study means results in some students not seeking support at all because they believe 'teachers won't care' (participant 3).

> *I feel that university study is mainly on our own . . . If we don't understand, we will try to find out the correct answer then try to figure it out ourselves*
> (participant 11).

Even if students know that independent learning is required, and understand what constitutes independent learning, barriers can still exist at the level of application. There are two main barriers at the application level: locating and accessing the support to succeed with learning independently. Both barriers can be attributed to multidimensional factors, such as having English as a second language, information overload, result-orientated tendency and differential previous experiences and customs. For example, participant 2 identified the need for support to become an independent learner, such as academic writing skills, time management skills and communication skills. They felt a lack of autonomy to locate this support and claimed that moving out of the small class environment within the IYO course made it harder to know who and how to ask for help. Interviewees explained that they do not pay attention to information or access support if they are not directly from their markers or related to assessment grades.

> *This kind of [academic skills support] email, everyone will selectively ignore, so it has caused us to miss such an opportunity*
> (participant 11).

The epistemological transition for Chinese students is ongoing (Dippold et al., 2022).

Language skills

Interviewees stated that they often felt more confident in preparatory courses, like the IYO course, because they perceived their language skills to be on an equal par with their international peers, and perceived tutors to be more able to understand non-native speakers of English than those tutors within the traditional, HE environment. One student reflected:

> *And then there is the International Year One class. If you ask questions your personal feeling is that you are feeling a little more relaxed. Then*

because I feel there are no language barriers, or less (barriers). In the business school there may be more language barriers because not all students and teachers are international

(participant 4).

Within the university, which has a less international focus than the IYO course, and is perceived to be less forgiving of making linguistic mistakes, students often feel self-conscious to speak, leading to a regression in their English communication skills (Dippold et al., 2022). For this reason, the transition process is a period when students can both lose and gain skills integral to succeeding in HE.

A recurrent theme that came from the interviews was the issue of valuable information being buried by an abundance of communication, particularly during induction. For non-native speakers of English, this level of communication can feel particularly overwhelming because of the time it takes to navigate English in a second language:

There is a lot of information which (I) feel is useless. When I need the information, for example, there is a total of 5 points of information. But I only need 1 point, but I must take the time to read the first 4 points, and then to find this 5th point. This is particularly wasted time. I will read until reaching the 3rd point. Then I will let the problem go without finding the solution

(participant 6).

To avoid students missing important information, interviewees were asked whether key headlines from induction information should be provided in the students' home language. All 13 interviewees thought this a good idea, with some students also recognising that this type of bi-lingual support is useful but should be limited to support the development of English language skills:

I think it will help if you add a little [Mandarin], but not too much because adding too much [Mandarin] will cause dependence

(participant 1).

As the interviewee emphasised, bilingual support is not simply translating everything into the student's home language. Instead, bilingual support should develop language learning and facilitate reciprocal adaptation, whereby both institution and student mutually adjust and progress through the transition process (Volet & Ang, 2012). Putting key headlines in the students' own language is not only practical for the retrieval of valuable information but may also help students develop a sense of belonging to the university which, through this bilingual approach, presents itself as an institution that welcomes diversity and celebrates the multiculturalism of its students.

Step 3: Developing the pre-arrival welcome pack[1]

The pre-arrival welcome pack was underpinned by research that suggests the transition process is a long-term one, where a students' home culture should be blended sympathetically with the culture of the UK HEI. As a result, the welcome pack was hosted on the University's virtual learning environment (VLE) but advertised via social media platforms that the students were already familiar with, such as WeChat. Using this platform for promotion allowed us to reach students on familiar ground, while inviting them onto a new platform that they would need to start using when studying at a UK university.

To ensure that the welcome pack was an effective transition tool, which met students on their own terms, it was co-created with two students from Chinese backgrounds. The co-creation not only helped produce a welcome pack relevant to real student needs but also demonstrated a commitment to creating an internationalised university.

The co-creation process

We worked with two final-year undergraduate international students online for four weeks. Bi-weekly, 90-minute online meetings were conducted. Additionally, the students each worked for an hour independently between sessions, creating material for the welcome pack, like videos, maps and study resources. The welcome pack was thoughtfully designed with particular emphasis on facilitating independent learning and providing language support to address transition challenges.

Independent learning

With careful consideration of the potential barriers for international students' independent learning, the first three stages of Bloom's taxonomy (Krathwohl, 2002) were employed to optimise the design of the welcome pack. At the 'remember' stage, a wide range of relevant and essential information was selected. Moving to the 'understanding' level, the focus was on addressing unknown unknowns and misunderstanding of independent learning, where students may not know what to expect or may misunderstand the concept of independent study leading to insufficient assistance. To mitigate these challenges, the welcome pack highlights the diverse range of academic and wellbeing support services that are readily accessible to all students free of charge (Figure 8.2).

At the 'application' level, the welcome pack facilitates students' autonomy to locate support by identifying key contacts and streamlining the support process. It also supports students' autonomy to access support by adopting a

---

1 The web link to the pre-arrival welcome pack: https://canvas.sussex.ac.uk/courses/21299

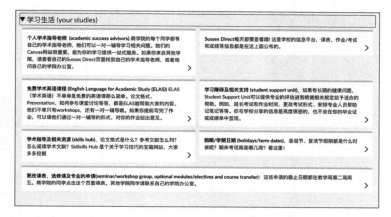

Figure 8.2 Example of the content provided in the 'your studies' section of the welcome pack

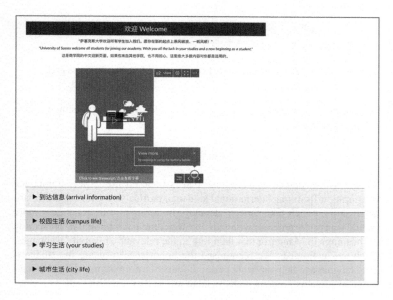

Figure 8.3 Example of the content overview of the welcome pack

holistic student-centred approach. It provides guidance tailored to different stages of the student transition journey (arriving, campus, study and city life), rather than employing the usual layout of fragmented departmental services (Figure 8.3). Thereby, academic support information is naturally integrated

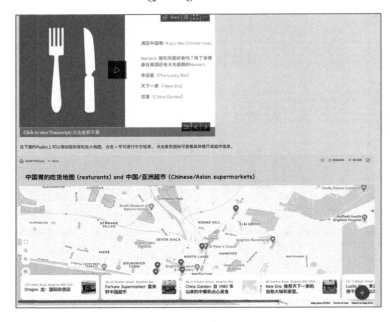

Figure 8.4 Example of a student-created videos and map for the welcome pack

into information on student life, such as career, living and socialising in a new culture (Figure 8.4).

Language skills

The interviews helped us recognise that we should not expect immediate acculturation from our international students, particularly with regard to language skills, which take time to develop. In an attempt to generate a more gradual transition process, we made the welcome pack bilingual, presenting key headings in Mandarin that then link to the relevant University webpages, which are in English. We recognised the importance of using the students' home language to help navigate large amounts of information, while also realising that students fundamentally need to utilise their English skills.

Impact of the pre-arrival welcome pack

The researchers conducted a small student survey one year after the publication of the welcome pack, and the feedback received was overwhelmingly positive. Out of 28 responders, all stated that they found the welcome pack helpful for their transition. Their comments confirmed the design intentions of the pack, highlighting where barriers of independent learning and language in transition had been minimised. The comprehensive and essential information was appreciated for contributing positively to their university experience. Furthermore, they found the clear and accessible home language headlines helpful when navigating through the university resources independently. One student also offered to help to improve the welcome pack in the survey, indicating enhanced student engagement and empowerment.

However, one student found it challenging to find the welcome pack's page, which led to infrequent visits. Overall, the survey results indicated that the welcome pack effectively served its purpose as a pre-arrival platform used to support international students' transition experiences.

Besides the positive feedback, students provided valuable suggestions for further improvements. Some students expressed a desire for more information related to mental health. One student suggested information about academic misconduct while another requested more information about academics' office hours. To address the feedback, researchers are updating the welcome pack with more extensive information. This survey will be conducted annually to fine-tune the welcome pack.

Recommendations

The findings from the interviews, the co-creation process, and the evaluation of the pre-arrival welcome pack, have helped us generate recommendations for other institutions looking to create a pre-arrival platform that supports international student transition into UK HE:

- Co-create material with current students from backgrounds that are similar to the target audience of your welcome pack (if your welcome pack is designed for a specific demographic), or from a variety of backgrounds (if you are creating a generic welcome pack for all incoming students).
- Use the co-creation element to, where possible, speak in the students' voice. If your welcome pack caters to native speakers of English, work with your students to help you avoid jargon and unnecessary academic language, so that your welcome pack is as clear as possible. In addition to this, if your welcome pack is designed for non-native speakers of English, consider ways in which you can make headline information bi-lingual, or even multi-lingual.
- Break information into small, manageable chunks.
- Consider both the academic and personal needs of your incoming cohort, creating a welcome pack that takes a holistic approach to transitioning into UK HE.
- Present information in a variety of ways, using video, text, audio, images etc.

- Think about the best place to host the welcome pack, locating it on a platform that is accessible to students not just pre-arrival but throughout the year.
- Where possible, advertise the welcome pack through channels that students are already familiar with. This will help with initial engagement.

References

Berman, R., & Cheng, L. (2001). English academic language skills: Perceived difficulties by undergraduate and graduate students, and their academic achievement. *Canadian Journal of Applied Linguistics, 4*(1), 25–40.

Cook-Sather, A., Bovill, C., & Felten, P. (2014). *Engaging students as partners in learning and teaching: A guide for faculty.* John Wiley & Sons.

Cotton, D. R., Joyner, M., George, R., & Cotton, P. A. (2016). Understanding the gender and ethnicity attainment gap in UK higher education. *Innovations in Education and Teaching International, 53*(5), 475–486.

Debray, C., & Spencer-Oatey, H. (2019). 'On the same page?' Marginalisation and positioning practices in intercultural teams. *Journal of Pragmatics, 144*, 15–28.

Dippold, D., Heron, M., & Gravett, K. (2022). International students' linguistic transitions into disciplinary studies: A rhizomatic perspective. *Higher Education, 83*(3), 527–545.

Dooey, P. (2010). Students' perspectives of an EAP pathway program. *Journal of English for Academic Purposes, 9*(3), 184–197.

Edwards, R. (1993). *Mature women students: Separating or connecting family and education.* Taylor & Francis.

Fraser, J., & Usman, M. (2021). Dreaming to learn together: Lessons in decolonial and anti-racist partnership practices. *The Journal of Educational Innovation, Partnership and Change, 7*(1).

Guyotte, K. W., Flint, M. A., & Latopolski, K. S. (2021). Cartographies of belonging: Mapping nomadic narratives of first-year students. *Critical Studies in Education, 62*(5), 543–558

Halic, O., Greenberg, K., & Paulus, T. (2009). Language and academic identity: A study of the experiences of non-native English speaking international students. *International Education, 38*(2), 73–93.

Hendrickson, B., Rosen, D., & Aune, R. K. (2011). An analysis of friendship networks, social connectedness, homesickness, and satisfaction levels of international students. *International Journal of Intercultural Relations, 35*(3), 281–295.

Jabbar, A., & Mirza, M. (2019). Managing diversity: Academic's perspective on culture and teaching. *Race Ethnicity and Education, 22*(5), 569–588

Kohan, N., Arabshahi, K. S., Mojtahedzadeh, R., Abbaszadeh, A., Rakhshani, T., & Emami, A. (2017). Self-directed learning barriers in a virtual environment: A qualitative study. *Journal of Advances in Medical Education & Professionalism, 5*(3), 116–123.

Krathwohl, D. R. (2002). A revision of Bloom's taxonomy: An overview. *Theory into Practice, 41*(4), 212–218.

Menzies, J. L., & Baron, R. (2014). International postgraduate student transition experiences: The importance of student societies and friends. *Innovations in Education and Teaching International, 51*(1), 84–94.

Moores, L., & Popadiuk, N. (2011). Positive aspects of international student transitions: A qualitative inquiry. *Journal of College Student Development, 52*(3), 291–306.

Ryan, J. (2011). Teaching and learning for international students: Towards a transcultural approach. *Teachers and Teaching, 17*(6), 631–648.

Ryan, J., & Viete, R. (2009). Respectful interactions: Learning with international students in the English-speaking academy. *Teaching in Higher Education, 14*(3), 303–314.

Sawir, E., Marginson, S., Deumert, A., Nyland, C., & Ramia, G. (2008). Loneliness and international students: An Australian study. *Journal of Studies in International Education, 12*(2), 148–180.

Sherry, M., Thomas, P., & Chui, W. H. (2010). International students: A vulnerable student population. *Higher Education, 60*, 33–46.

Smith, S. (2020, February 20). What about me? International student attainment in UK higher education. *HEPI.* Retrieved April 28, 2023, from www.hepi.ac.uk/2020/02/20/what-about-me-international-student-attainment-in-uk-higher-education/

Sovic, S. (2012). Classroom encounters: International students' perceptions of tutors in the creative arts. In *International students negotiating higher education* (pp. 87–103). Routledge.

Thomas, L. (2012). Building student engagement and belonging in Higher Education at a time of change. *Paul Hamlyn Foundation, 100*(1–99). www.phf.org.uk/wp-content/uploads/2014/10/What-Works-Summary-report.pdf

Tian, M., & Lowe, J. A. (2014). Intercultural identity and intercultural experiences of American students in China. *Journal of Studies in International Education, 18*(3), 281–297.

Tran, L. T. (2020). Teaching and engaging international students: People-to-people empathy and people-to-people connections. *Journal of International Students, 10*(3), xii–xvii.

Volet, S. E., & Ang, G. (2012). Culturally mixed groups on international campuses: An opportunity for inter-cultural learning. *Higher Education Research & Development, 31*(1), 21–37.

Willis, I., & Sedghi, G. (2014). Perceptions and experiences of home students involved in welcoming and supporting direct entry 2nd year international students. *Practice and Evidence of Scholarship of Teaching and Learning in Higher Education, 9*(1), 2–17.

Yakunina, E. S., Weigold, I. K., Weigold, A., Hercegovac, S., & Elsayed, N. (2013). International students' personal and multicultural strengths: Reducing acculturative stress and promoting adjustment. *Journal of Counseling & Development, 91*(2), 216–223.

9 Screening and data collection in pre-arrival platforms

Rebecca Wilson

This chapter explores screening and collecting information from students as part of pre-arrival platforms to support students' transitions to higher education. It focuses on collecting large quantities of data across the student population but also considers data collection from individual students. It explores information on student expectations and reflections captured during this data collection and how this can be used to provide tailored feedback to students, using the Transitions Toolkit, a pre-arrival platform at the University of St Andrews, as a case study.

The Transitions Toolkit is an interactive survey with two iterations: one for UG students and one for PGT students. The objective of these toolkits is to enable critical self-reflection in preparation for students' arrival at university. The toolkit is designed to provide students with an understanding of studying at higher education level while gathering information about their expectations, which can be implemented in further transition initiatives.

Case study – the transitions toolkit

At the University of St Andrews, our pre-arrival platform, the Transitions Toolkit, is delivered through survey software Qualtrics. This pre-arrival survey was created as a proactive response to overcome the recurring problem of students' mismatched expectations, particularly around academic experience.

The Transitions Toolkit was developed from the QAA Enhancement Theme 'student transitions', which ran from 2014 to 2017. In order to give all new entrants to the university the option to engage with pre-arrival support, an online survey or platform was identified. The platform was created in conjunction with academic schools and researchers in the School of Psychology to create an interactive reflective tool, which enabled us to provide immediate tailored feedback to students while collecting information on their expectations. In the toolkit, students are given the opportunity to answer questions that were created in conjunction with academic departments and, therefore, are targeted to consider both general and subject-specific skills and

DOI: 10.4324/9781003427575-13

experiences. The questions relate to motivations for coming to university, expectations, independent learning and critical thinking and approaches to study. Students have the ability to select their academic school(s) to answer subject-specific questions on independent learning, critical thinking, and other university skills. Automated subject-specific examples are then supplied to students based on these answers to highlight the skills needed, such as what critical thinking in the subject of History entails or what to expect in Biology lab sessions.

The Transitions Toolkit has three aims:

1. to provide students with an insight into university level study before they arrive
2. to gather key information about their expectations
3. to stimulate students to critically self-reflect in preparation for this transition

The results from the pre-arrival platform are shared across departments and used to implement effective learning strategies and personalise inductions based on students' contributions. External to direct student experience, results from this toolkit have facilitated further pedagogical research into student learning identities and student experience.

At the University of St Andrews, our pre-arrival survey is divided into five blocks:

Introduction: introducing the survey and gathering basic and demographic information, such as gender identity, age and recent education experience. This information is collected as the survey is anonymous and thus is used to analyse results using these categories.
Learning approach: exploring how students will approach learning and their expectations of university. Topics include students' understanding of terms such as critical thinking and independent learning. School-specific answers are generated from these questions.
Studying: exploring specific study skills such as time management and using feedback from lecturers. This section also explores the specifics of studying at St Andrews, such as using the library, virtual learning environments and expectations in tutorials.
School specific: here schools have the option to add additional questions, such as expectations of working in a biology lab, for example, or how students engage with current affairs in International Relations.
Close: the survey is closed, and students have the opportunity to share essential feedback on the survey.

The toolkit is distributed by email, through which an invitation to complete the toolkit is shared, via our registration team, to all incoming students who have received an unconditional confirmed offer. The distribution starts in June, although a large portion of invitations are not sent until after A-Level, IB, and Scottish Higher results are announced in August. The Toolkit closes before Orientation Week and results are quickly generated and distributed to schools across the University to analyse and implement necessary measures to help students. A more thorough report which analyses patterns is created and distributed later in semester one.

The primary objective of the University of St Andrews pre-arrival platform is to help manage students' expectations of being a student in higher education. This is helpful for all students, including those who are returning to education after a long time away, or those coming straight from school. The toolkit explores what they think being a university student involves, in addition to providing automatic and tailored responses to their responses. For example, when looking at one of the most challenging aspects of being a university student, studying autonomously, we ask the question: 'what does independent study mean to you?' Then, an automated response, based on the specific subject area they selected, will be generated to help guide them on what the university and their subject understands independent learning to be. This forms part of their long induction process which is reinforced in orientation week and throughout their first semester (and year) of study.

This system has a dual benefit as we are able to then collect responses from students and these expectations are then shared with staff members in their school, as well as those who support learning and teaching, to implement effective mechanisms of support. For example, the central learning and teaching unit, Centre for Educational Enhancement and Development (CEED), runs an effective study skills session that is open to all new UG students in Orientation week. This session is tailored based upon the answers in our pre-arrival platform at the beginning of each year. This makes sure that the session is targeting what students would like to cover while also normalising students' concerns. Here, we share the patterns of students' answers to highlight similarities and show that most students are nervous about starting university or are unsure and how they will manage their time.

Creating/updating a platform to include data collection or screening

By incorporating a data collection or screening element into your pre-arrival platform, you have the unique opportunity to tailor student learning and shape expectations based on your own students' insights. This could be a broad overview of collective expectations of the incoming student body or a focus on the individual student's needs.

When designing a pre-arrival platform which has a data collection aspect, the aims of the data collection are vital to ensure an effective and useful platform. It is crucial to reflect on what your own institution's (or department's) aims for the survey are. These aims could include:

1. Screening students for additional learning needs
2. Creating a learning profile for individual students
3. Outlining student expectations at the discipline or institution level
4. Highlighting students' concerns for the upcoming academic year
5. Evaluating students' approaches to learning
6. Appraising students' awareness of core concepts

As part of the transition to higher education, collecting student information prior to their arrival at university enables you to adapt current programmes or personalise learning support plans.

Another step in reflecting on the aims of your platform is to consider who will receive the data collected by the platform. This could be members of the student learning team, lecturers across the institution, personal tutors or the students themselves. Based on the intended outcomes and aims of the data collection, it is important to choose software that enables you to achieve these goals. If a pre-arrival platform already exists, the software employed may have the option to add a survey feature, as is the case with many VLEs. Though when creating a platform from scratch, you may wish to use specialist survey software in order to tailor data collection to your needs.

A very important consideration when designing a survey is whether to make it anonymous or not. By linking the answers to a student, you have the option to share specific details and expectations to their learning team and lecturers. For example, some universities will share the answers to a pre-arrival platform with personal tutors. Others will use the platform to identify specific learning differences or other challenges to learning, which would not be possible if the survey was anonymous.

However, there are also benefits to using anonymity in surveys; most notably students are more honest in their answers (Thomas, 2017). Thus, you have a greater insight into students' expectations. This model is used at the University of St Andrews, where, instead of focusing on individual responses, we look at university-wide and subject-specific concerns and reflections.

It is important to consider how the platform will be distributed as this will have a significant impact on completion rates (although it is hoped that all students will engage with the pre-arrival materials). Many universities choose to include the platform within other matriculation materials or information shared once students have accepted an offer.

To summarise, steps in creating or updating a platform to include data collection or screening involve:

1. Reflecting on the aims of the data collection/ screening
2. Reflecting on who will receive the data collected

3. Selecting the correct software for the data collection
4. Choosing whether the data collection will remain anonymous
5. Explore how the platform will be distributed

Benefits

Collecting information in a pre-arrival platform is a time-effective way to learn more about the incoming student population, while highlighting any issues that they may face. There are many benefits to collecting data or screening in a pre-arrival platform. One of the largest is the efficiency of collecting data from a large proportion of incoming students; there may be few other times when all students are engaging in a platform that has the option of aggregating information at such a scale.

The timing of the data collection and screening is also of great benefit to the transition to university process. At the individual level, this affords students the opportunity to reflect on the upcoming change and possibly receive individualised feedback and support to aid this transition. At an institutional level, this provides an overview for the thoughts of students before arriving at the university.

A focus on student expectations during transition is vital as these expectations have a significant impact on the success of students at university, especially their learning experiences (Biggs, 1996). This system of exploring expectations enables students to reflect on their past and upcoming experiences, while highlighting the key challenges and concerns students have to staff within the institutions.

Another benefit of collecting information in a pre-arrival platform is to screen for any possible additional learning needs. This is a model many universities adopt, as screening can highlight specific learning differences, such as dyslexia, dyspraxia, and ADHD, alerting staff members to follow-up with these students to provide any additional support that may be required. This system of screening can also be used to identify long-term health conditions that students may not have disclosed or other factors that may act as barriers to learning. This method of screening is far more valuable when associated with an identifier on the survey, such as a name or student number.

Challenges

There are several challenges to be aware of when using screening in pre-arrival platforms.

As there is a likelihood that you will be collecting highly sensitive data, including information on disability, race or gender, there is a need to ensure that GDPR (General Data Protection Regulations) procedures are in place. Here, choosing the correct software and systems is imperative. This means that no laws or rules will be broken, but also students' data are secure.

Beyond this practicality, a challenge that can be harder to mitigate is students' perception of the pre-arrival platform. When gathering information, they may be concerned there is a 'correct' answer or an answer that university is wanting to see more than others. Similarly, as with any research, the question type will have an impact on the answer students share. For example, the question 'How do you feel about attending university?' will produce a different answer to 'do you feel nervous about attending university?' or 'are you excited about attending university?'

While, in principle, good research methodology would discourage us from using leading questions, such as the latter two, there is benefit to collecting quantitative data from these types of questions, e.g. obtaining a percentage of students who feel nervous about attending university. It also occupies less of the pre-arrival platform team's time to process these data, compared to qualitative questions. Here, the aim of each question is important, and the author needs to reflect on how the wording of the question may trigger different responses from different students.

Furthermore, students may face survey or information fatigue. If they receive a large amount of information before arriving at university, they may become overwhelmed and refrain from engaging with these questionnaires. This is especially true if the system is hard to navigate or there are many steps to complete, for example, if a student needs to have completed a matriculation step and have received/activated a university email account prior to accessing the platform. While some procedures may be essential to ensure that only students who are attending the university will complete the survey, reflecting on barriers to using the platform can produce a higher completion rate and enable students from diverse backgrounds to engage. This may include giving simple instructions on the best way to engage with the platform, e.g. is it accessible on a phone.

Systems to navigate challenges

- Choose the correct software and systems to comply with GDPR
- Explain the aims of the survey/ data collection, highlighting there are no right or wrong answers
- Reflect on the purpose of the questions
- Think of technology barriers to engagement with the platform

Conclusion

Data collection in pre-arrival platforms is an effective way to gain insight into incoming student bodies. Based upon the aims of the institution, this data collection can be tailored to shape student learning and programmes in the transition period. Whether looking at broad student expectations or focusing on individual student needs, data collection is a quick way to implement new learning initiatives. Placing student expectations at the heart of this data collection will enable you to shape services accordingly, as well as enabling students to reflect on these expectations.

This chapter explored data collection and screening in pre-arrival platforms; first, by outlining the Transitions Toolkit (a pre-arrival platform developed and implemented by the University of St Andrews) and the outcomes of this project. It then examined the many benefits and challenges of data collection in transitions projects and reinforced them by looking at the logistics of implementing this into a new or existing platform.

References

Biggs, J. (1996). Enhancing teaching through constructive alignment. *Higher Education, 32*(3), 347–364.

Thomas, G. (2017). *Doing research.* Palgrave.

10 Supporting mature students in transition using pre-arrival platforms

Steve Russell

What *is* a mature student? In a higher education setting, it is defined as those who are over the age of 21 at the commencement of studies and have returned to education after a significant period away from formal education or have never pursued higher education before, based on the UK Parliamentary briefing paper by Hubble and Bolton (2021). These students bring a wealth of experience and perspectives to the academic community, but they also face unique challenges in their pursuit of a degree (O'Donnell & Tobbell, 2007). There are several reasons why widening participation of mature students is important. First, it provides opportunities for individuals who may have missed out on higher education earlier in life to gain new skills and knowledge that can help them advance in their careers. Second, it can help to address skills shortages in certain industries, as mature students may bring valuable work experience and a diverse perspective to the classroom. Wilson (1997) for example points to their greater life experience as a particular asset and Jackson and Jamieson (2009) point to the development of foundation degrees to help fill skills shortages in industry. Finally, it can also help to promote social mobility and reduce inequalities in access to higher education (see Bathmaker et al., 2016 for a discussion of social mobility and education).

According to Hubble and Bolton (2021), in their UK Parliament Research Briefing paper, the number of mature students in England has decreased from over 400k in 2010/11 to fewer than 240k in 2017/18. This has largely been driven by a reduction in part-time courses. In 2019–2020 for example, Hubble and Bolton report that 28% of mature students starting a first degree are registered part-time compared to only 3% of younger students.

According to the Office for Students, mature students are more likely to be from underrepresented or disadvantaged groups, more likely to be Black, Asian or Minority Ethnic, have known disabilities, and have non-traditional qualifications than younger students. It has also been shown that mature students are more likely to drop out of their course than younger students. In 2017–2018, 84% of full-time mature students continued onto their second year of study compared to 92% for young students. The continuation rate for

DOI: 10.4324/9781003427575-14

mature part-time students was also lower than that for young students (Office for Students, 2021).

Mature students on full-time courses have poorer degree outcomes than young students. In 2018–2019, 70.3% of full-time mature students graduated with a 1st or 2:1 compared to 80.2% of young students. In contrast, part-time mature students achieve better outcomes compared to younger part-time students. In 2018–19, 61.3% of mature part-time students achieved a 1st or a 2.1 compared to only 44.4% of young part-time students (Office for Students, 2021).

Why is there the concern over a small number of students when there are competing needs in teaching a whole cohort? Mature students bring so many advantages to higher education: They often have more life experience and a broader perspective on the world, which can enrich classroom discussions and contribute to a more diverse academic community. They may also have well-developed skills such as time management, communication, and problem-solving, which can help them succeed academically and in their future careers if we get the support and transition process right. Participation in learning can have enormous benefits for mature students in terms of self-fulfilment as well as civic engagement and health and family functioning (Swain & Hammond, 2011). For society, adults who have engaged with learning are more likely to be in employment than not (Jenkins et al., 2002).

Specific challenges for mature students transitioning into university settings

Competing responsibilities

One significant challenge for mature students is balancing their academic commitments with their other responsibilities, such as work, family and career responsibilities (Fambely, 2020). Many mature students have jobs and families and may need to juggle these responsibilities with their coursework and study time. Chapman (2011) points to the high social, financial and personal risk that can often accompany Higher Education study for mature students. This can be especially challenging for those pursuing full-time programmes, which can require a significant time commitment. Swain and Hammond (2011) reported that having young children, unsupportive partners, high-pressure jobs or health problems were all significant constraints affecting the learning of mature students disproportionately. This has the potential to impact students meeting deadlines leading to the struggle to get evidence for extenuating circumstances appeals and failing to meet learning outcomes for exam boards, leading to deferral and or poor experience. Historically, personal or financial reasons have been significant factors in the decision of mature students to withdraw from higher education (Lucas & Ward, 1985).

Academic culture

Many mature students have been away from formal education for a number of years and may find the academic culture, expectations and technology unfamiliar or overwhelming. They may sense a skills deficit as described by Dearnley et al. (2006) or as Roberts and Higgins (1992) suggest, it may be because of the lack of practice associated with learning. Familiarity with digital tools and platforms that are now commonplace in higher education is likely to need attention. Staddon (2020) for example reported that mature students use fewer technologies than younger students and use them less frequently.

Student support

To support mature students in higher education, universities and colleges can provide a range of services and resources, such as academic advising, tutoring and study skills workshops.

Expectations

Mature students will have varied backgrounds and experiences: Mature students come from diverse backgrounds and may have very different experiences, which can make it challenging to find common ground and create a cohesive learning environment (Benson, 2022). Mature students may have different approaches to learning compared to younger students. They may benefit from a more hands-on, experiential learning opportunities or may prefer a more self-directed approach to learning. Ultimately mature students may have different expectations for their education than younger students. They may be more focused on developing practical skills or advancing their careers and may be less interested in traditional academic pursuits.

Transition strategies to meet mature student challenges

Here are some strategies that universities and policymakers can use to help widen participation of mature students in higher education:

1. **Outreach and support**: Universities can work to reach out to mature students and provide support throughout the application and enrolment process. This may include targeted marketing and outreach campaigns, as well as dedicated staff or services to provide advice and support (TASO, 2021).
2. **Flexible learning:** Offering flexible learning options such as part-time, evening or online courses can help to make higher education more accessible to mature students. As a response to the COVID-19 pandemic many

institutions have improved online provision using well-produced asynchronous material, and this offers flexibility in learning (UCAS, 2021). They can also offer flexible course scheduling, such as evening and weekend classes or online courses, to accommodate the needs of students with other commitments (Bolam & Dodgson, 2003).

3. **Financial support:** Universities and policymakers can offer financial support such as scholarships, grants or loans to help cover the costs of tuition, living expenses or childcare (Sorella, 2022).

4. **Recognition of prior learning:** Mature students may have valuable work experience or other qualifications that can be recognised for credit towards a degree program. Universities can work to develop policies and procedures to recognise and credit prior learning (TASO, 2021).

5. **Mentorship and peer support:** Universities can provide mentorship and peer support programmes to help mature students adjust to university life and connect with other students who may be in similar situations (TASO, 2021). In addition, universities can create support networks for mature students, such as peer mentoring programmes and student organisations, to help them connect with other students who are in similar situations and, as with all underrepresented groups in higher education, have a voice and be heard.

6. **Degree apprenticeships:** Offering degree apprenticeships to mature students will provide them with a paid role and the experience outside of the classroom, but this does mean building relationships with stakeholders, training providers and training staff around the standards required of apprenticeships (Office for Students, 2023).

What pre-arrival platforms can add?

Rather than simply relying on initiatives that can be implemented during induction and beyond, setting students up to succeed from their start of their journey in higher education using pre-arrival platforms can be particularly beneficial for mature students in several ways:

1. Information and resources: Pre-arrival platforms can provide mature students with information about the academic requirements of their chosen degree program. This can help them better understand the coursework and expectations of the program, which can be helpful in preparing for their studies. Additionally, these platforms may provide information on financial aid, course options, academic support services and campus resources, making it easier for mature students to navigate the university experience (HESA, 2023).

2. Preparation: Returning to education after a break can be daunting, especially for mature students who may have additional responsibilities such as work and family commitments. Pre-arrival platforms can provide

information on university life and what to expect, including campus resources, extracurricular activities and time management strategies.
3. Support and networking opportunities: Pre-arrival platforms can connect mature students with others who are preparing to return to education, as well as alumni, faculty and staff who can offer support and guidance. This can be particularly helpful for mature students who may feel isolated or unsure about their decision to return to education.
4. Increased confidence: Accessing pre-arrival platforms can help mature students build confidence in their decision to return to education. By providing information, resources and support, these platforms can help mature students feel better prepared for the challenges of college life and more confident in their ability to succeed.

By providing information, support and networking opportunities, these platforms can help mature students succeed in their academic journey.

Generic examples of pre-arrival platforms for mature students include:

1. College for Adults (https://collegeforadults.org). This US platform provides information and resources for adults who are considering returning to college. It includes information on financial aid, course options and academic support services.
2. UK government (www.gov.uk/mature-student-university-funding). This website offers a comprehensive guide for adults who are considering returning to education. It includes information on financial aid, career options and study strategies.
3. Return to Learn (www.nidirect.gov.uk/articles/returning-learning). This platform provides resources for adults who are considering returning to education, including information on degree programmes, scholarships and time management strategies.

At my own institute, Aston University, although we have quite a small number of mature students compared with universities of similar size and standing in the university rankings, we do offer several pre-arrival platforms and resources for mature students who are considering returning to education. Here are some examples:

1. Mature Students' Guide: The Mature Students' Guide provides information on returning to education as a mature student, including advice on funding, study skills and support services available at Aston University. The guide is available on the university website.
2. Personalised advice and guidance: Mature students can access personalised advice and guidance from a Mature Students' Adviser. The adviser can offer guidance on course selection, finance, and support services, and can also put mature students in touch with other support services within the university.

3. Online resources: A range of online resources to support mature students in their academic journey include study skills workshops, online forums and webinars on topics such as time management, exam preparation and essay writing.
4. Pre-arrival events: Pre-arrival events for mature students provide an opportunity to meet other mature students and staff, and to find out more about the university's support services.
5. Accommodation options: Aston University offers dedicated mature student accommodation options. This accommodation is designed to meet the specific needs of mature students and is in a quieter area of the campus.

Conclusion

Mature students in higher education face unique challenges, but they also bring valuable perspectives and experiences to the academic community. By providing targeted support and resources, universities can help these students succeed and contribute to a more diverse and dynamic higher education environment.

By implementing some of these strategies, universities and policymakers can help to widen participation of mature students in higher education and promote greater access to educational opportunities for all. This means providing funding, training for tutors and recognition that all students will have their own identity and background impacting their learning journey and that lessons learnt from engaging with different educational stakeholders will impact all students for the better.

References

Bathmaker, A. M., Ingram, N., Abrahams, J., Hoare, A., Waller, R., & Bradley, H. (2016). *Higher education, social class and social mobility: The degree generation.* Springer.

Benson, T. (2022). *Universities must remove barriers facing access to HE students.* WONKHE. Retrieved May 16, 2023, from https://wonkhe.com/blogs/universities-must-remove-the-barriers-facing-access-to-he-students/

Bolam, H., & Dodgson, R. (2003). Retaining and supporting mature students in higher education. *Journal of Adult and Continuing Education, 8*(2), 179–194.

Chapman, A. (2011). *Mature students' transition to higher education: A (re)negotiation of identity and of becoming a 'novice academic'* [Doctoral dissertation, Lancaster University].

Dearnley, C., Dunn, G., & Watson, S. (2006). An exploration of on-line access by non-traditional students in higher education: A case study. *Nurse Education Today, 26*(5), 409–415.

Fambely, C. A. (2020). Committed to yourself or have yourself committed: Balancing family life with student success. *Canadian Journal of Dental Hygiene, 54*(1), 16.

HESA. (2023). *Higher education student statistics: UK 2021/22.* Retrieved October 29, 2023, from www.hesa.ac.uk/news/19-01-2023/sb265-higher-education-student-statistics.

Hubble and Bolton. (2021, February 24). *Mature higher education students in England.* House of Commons Briefing Paper Number 8809. https://commonslibrary.parliament.uk/research-briefings/cbp-8809/

Jackson, S., & Jamieson, A. (2009). Higher education, mature students and employment goals: Policies and practices in the UK. *Journal of Vocational Education and Training, 61*(4), 399–411.

Jenkins, A., VIignoles, A., Wolf, A., & Galindo-Rueda, F. (2002). *The determinants and effects of lifelong learning.* Centre for the Economics of Education Discussion Paper, CEEDP019.

Lucas, S., & Ward, P. (1985). Mature students at Lancaster University. *Adult Education (London), 58*(2), 151–157.

O'Donnell, V. L., & Tobbell, J. (2007). The transition of adult students to higher education: Legitimate peripheral participation in a community of practice? *Adult Education Quarterly, 57*(4), 312–328.

Office for Students. (2021). *Improving opportunity and choice for mature students.* www.officeforstudents.org.uk/publications/improving-opportunity-and-choice-for-mature-students/

Office for Students. (2023). *Degree apprenticeships: A viable alternative?* www.officeforstudents.org.uk/publications/degree-apprenticeships-a-viable-alternative

Roberts, D., Higgins, T. & Lloyd, R. (1992). *Higher Education: The student experience: the findings of a research programme into the views and experiences of students in higher education.* Heist.

Sorella. (2022). Mature students in universities face 3 kinds of barriers – here's how to address them. *The Conversation.* Retrieved May 17, 2023, from https://theconversation.com/mature-students-in-universities-face-3-kinds-of-barriers-heres-how-to-address-them-180389.

Staddon, R. V. (2020). Bringing technology to the mature classroom: Age differences in use and attitudes. *International Journal of Educational Technology in Higher Education, 17*(1), 1–20.

Swain, J., & Hammond, C. (2011). The motivations and outcomes of studying for part-time mature students in higher education. *International Journal of Lifelong Education, 30*(5), 591–612.

TASO. (2021). *Supporting access and student success for mature learners.* https://taso.org.uk/wp-content/uploads/TASO-mature-students-summary-report-2021.pdf

UCAS. (2021). Retrieved May 17, 2023, from www.ucas.com/undergraduate/applying-university/undergraduate-individual-needs/mature-students

Wilson, F. (1997). The construction of paradox? One case of mature students in higher education. *Higher Education Quarterly, 51*(4), 347–366.

11 Supporting students with non-traditional entry qualifications

Peter Alston, Dawne Irving-Bell, Claire Stocks, Sarah McIlroy and David Wooff

In this chapter, we explore the role of pre-arrival activity designed to support learners to become 'academically ready' for higher education study. To begin, the chapter defines 'pre-arrival', before moving to offer an overview of the potential challenges students may face. Having presented for discussion several pre-arrival strategies, to articulate their value, rather than describing the benefits in isolation of those who experience them, crafted from conversations with students, the chapter shares their stories. Drawing on perceptions of their lived experience, we use their voices to illustrate the unique value of these approaches and their impact in practice. Exemplifying how, through these opportunities, students have not just been supported from offer to arrival, but also how the pre-arrival support has been instrumental in equipping them with skills, knowledge and understanding, facilitating their ability to progress through their studies with confidence; enabling them to excel, and to thrive in higher education. To close, the chapter draws together key features of successful pre-arrival approaches together and signposts you, the reader, to further research and resources.

What 'pre-arrival' entails and the need to consider non-traditional learners

Pre-arrival strategies are practical actions designed to help learners transition smoothly into their new academic environment. Within the context of this chapter, 'pre-arrival' refers to a package of workshops, online resources, and face-to-face support to help learners develop a range of essential academic skills. Approaches, methods and mechanisms are designed specifically to facilitate access, provide resources, information and any other activity that supports students in the liminal space that falls between the point at which an offer is made and formal study begins.

It is worth spending a few minutes to explain why, within the context of traditional and non-traditional learners, this work is important. The success of every student is of paramount importance. Recognising the value of a diverse student population, and to support learners and maintain Office for

DOI: 10.4324/9781003427575-15

Students (OfS) conditions of registration, providers have become increasingly creative and flexible in their approaches to improve equality of opportunity for underrepresented groups to access, succeed in, and progress through higher education.

Alongside the development of innovative, alternative entry routes, many institutions are working to implement unique approaches to support learners at every stage of interaction on their higher education journey. Embedding these strategies to support all learners and maintain conditions of registration is crucial.

For example, they can play an important role in supporting undergraduate mature students who, according to Bolton (2023) and Bolton and Lewis (2023), are more likely to drop out of higher education than their younger counterparts. (For reference according to UCAS (2023), the term 'mature student' refers to students over the age of 21 at the start of an undergraduate degree, or over 25 years of age at the beginning of a postgraduate programme.) Or they may be particularly helpful for women who are more likely to be mature students, or black female students, 41% of whom were mature learners in 2020 according to Hubble and Bolton (2021).

The challenges

Accessing higher education can pose several challenges for students. The shift to a new academic setting can be daunting, even for learners moving directly from further education. In this section we present a summary of the challenges that non-traditional students in particular, may face:

Financial constraints and external obligations: Financial barriers can pose a significant challenge for any student. Additional challenges may be faced by learners without traditional qualifications because they may be ineligible for certain scholarships, for example those tied to specific academic achievements, hence making funding acquisition a little more difficult. Mature learners may face financial barriers due to existing responsibilities such as work and/or family obligations, which can make it tough to balance their educational pursuits with other responsibilities.

Academic preparedness: Depending upon the length of time since their last educational experience, additional academic support to refresh or develop new academic skills to bridge gaps may be required. For learners returning to education, there may be additional challenges in adapting to the use of new educational technology. Additional support to develop digital literacy and navigate the online tools and resources used in higher education may also be required.

Social and cultural adjustment: Students with non-traditional academic backgrounds may feel a sense of imposter syndrome or experience a lack of confidence due to not following a conventional learning path. Some learners may be anxious or apprehensive about their abilities to succeed academically, or harbour concerns around assimilation into a new culture. Mature learners may face additional challenges due to the age difference and may feel isolated or find it difficult to connect with their peers, to participate in extracurricular or study group activities.

Preparing students for successful study

Having illuminated the challenges, we present for discussion successful pre-arrival strategies designed specifically to help remove barriers and offer targeted support and assist learners' smooth transition into higher education.

Typically, this support, which is optional and incurs no student fee, is delivered over several weeks prior to a student starting university. Mindful that students with non-traditional entry qualifications may be particularly apprehensive about returning to study, or want to get a head start, to help them juggle work alongside childcare, or other responsibilities, institutions are mindful to ensure that the strategies offered provide opportunities to study in a way that fits around students' external commitments (OfS, 2021).

Pre-arrival checklist, information and guidance

An increasing number of institutions provide a dedicated 'before you arrive' web page to support incoming students. Typically, communication signposts students to information about accommodation choices, financial support, health and safety, registration and other important aspects of studying at the institution. For example, course selection or academic planning. Where institutions have international students, institutions may also provide a 'pre-arrival' checklist to help ensure students complete all necessary preparations. Typically, this support includes pre-departure guidance and information to aid students to secure accommodation, obtain documentation (e.g. visas), set up a bank account or secure mobile phone service. As advocated by The British Council (2020), some institutions also offer additional support which may include a 'meet and greet' service, new-arrival help desks for international students and free transport to university accommodation.

Orientation

To help students to settle in, and create a sense of belonging, orientation has long been an established feature of student induction, providing students with materials to support integration into campus life, academic programmes, student and learning services and extracurricular activities. However, in recent years, institutions have become increasingly creative, and many offer these activities as part of their pre-arrival platforms to help ensure students get off to a flying start. In addition to orientation activity designed to support students to navigate virtual spaces, a number use technology, including video and live streaming, to help students navigate physical spaces, including campus facilities and accommodation.

Online communities, peer support and mentoring

Providing insights into both the academic and social aspects of life at the institution can help ease concerns. A feature of successful pre-arrival platforms is the facilitation of networking, enabling students, to make connections with current ones and sometimes alumni before arriving on campus. For example, pre-arrival platforms can be used to facilitate engagement with online communities where incoming students can connect with each other, ask questions and share their experiences. Activity of this nature can help foster a sense of belonging and provide peer support before students begin their studies.

Language and cultural preparation

Emphasising support for equality, diversity and inclusion (EDI), as part of their package of support, institutions may offer pre-arrival tasks designed to develop academic skills where English may not be the learners' first language. Language and cultural preparation may also feature learning materials and resources for language proficiency or equivalency assessments and include support to students adjusting to a new cultural context.

Developing academic study skills

Mindful of the diversity in learner background, a key feature of all pre-arrival platforms are strategies that focus on preparation for study. Even students moving directly from further education need support to acclimatise to new approaches they will face. Work to develop academic preparedness frequently focuses on developing study skills to help ensure students have the skills and knowledge they need to succeed in higher education. Typically, activity includes strategies to support effective reading, and academic writing skills. With a focus on 'learning to learn', many pre-arrival platforms feature integral workshops designed to support learners with time management, organisation, and planning. In addition to academic reading and writing skills, tasks may encourage students to explore diverse approaches to study, or receive support to develop often-overlooked skills, such as note taking or and revision techniques. They may also be encouraged to engage in activities that will help them become familiar with other approaches, such as sketch noting or poster presentations (Irving-Bell, 2019; Irving-Bell & Hartley, 2022).

To scaffold future development and build confidence, activity may model a variety of pedagogical practices designed to introduce students to multiple learning approaches. For example, alongside traditional style lectures, seminars and online learning, some pre-arrival work may offer opportunities for students to engage in present-in-person teaching, active learning (Betts & Oprandi, 2022) or role play or simulation (Chernikova et al., 2020).

Learning technology

Starting with basic computer skills, fundamental features of many pre-access platforms include an introduction to Microsoft Office, and tasks designed to help students to become familiar with their respective university's systems, providing support for even the most 'tech savvy' students. For example, navigating the online learning environment, synchronising personal devices to ensure secure access, and accessing papers, journals and books electronically. An additional benefit of this support at this early juncture is the ability to assess individual students' IT capability or personal requirements such as accessing assistive technologies. Furthermore, needs can also be appraised; to determine if the student has access to suitable technological equipment, they may need to complete their studies.

Case studies

We share two case studies featuring student perceptions to illustrate how the use of such pre-arrival support has helped students with non-traditional entry qualifications to achieve their academic goals. These are presented as vignettes. Vignettes are a well-established method for collecting data in social science research (Finch, 1987). They have been used to explore a wide range of topics, generate rich data, and allow researchers to gain an insider perspective on the topic being studied. In this study, we draw upon the concept of real-life vignettes (Sampson & Johannessen, 2020; Gray et al., 2017) to present short, fictionalised accounts based upon actual, typical participant accounts. These allow research participants to share their experiences, perspectives and understandings of the impact of their higher education pre-arrival access and transition activity.

Case study 1: Ryland

English was not Ryland's first language, which coupled with dyslexia made it hard for him to learn in a traditional classroom setting. He left compulsory education without qualifications, but he never stopped loving learning. Working as an equestrian, he found his passion for teaching while working with children and young people at the stables. Ryland decided he wanted to explore a career in teaching. Having completed an access programme, Ryland was offered support to pass university equivalency tests in mathematics and English and subsequently secured his place on an Undergraduate Initial Teacher Education course. In advance of his studies, Ryland took advantage of his institution's pre-arrival platform and received a package of support designed to aid his transition into higher education.

How the pre-arrival support helped

Before embarking upon his studies, apprehensive about the transition into higher education Ryland took advantage of his university's pre-arrival support which included activity designed to build confidence and support students where English is not their first language.

> *From the start the tutors did everything to make me feel at ease. I had a menu of tasks I could choose from, with guidance about which workshops may be most useful to me. There were a range of face-to-face and virtual support sessions designed to help develop my academic skills and build my confidence. I remember my first was an informal 'ice breaker' where I was able to meet other students. In another, the skills advisor took time to help everyone to become familiar with university 'dos and don'ts'. Adopting an informal approach helped establish a comfortable and safe environment. Everyone felt able to participate, without feeling judged.*
>
> *The sessions included mock assignments, support for academic reading, referencing, and guidance on preparing presentations. The workshops also gave advice to help me to manage my time, meet deadlines and tips to maintain a good study-life balance. The teaching approaches used included discussion, paired and group work. I found some activities to be quite demanding, but I was supported at every stage. As I completed each activity, I could feel myself growing in confidence, knowing I was being prepared to begin my degree.*
>
> *When I started my degree, things I learnt during pre-arrival helped me to settle into university life. For example, knowing where to find and how to access online learning tools to find academic information. One task required us to submit a piece of work into Turnitin, the plagiarism detection software. Turnitin is used to generate similarity reports, but we were also shown how we could use it following submission to help paraphrase and reference more accurately. This gave me a real advantage when I started my degree.*

While it may seem early, some platforms encourage learners to think about and provide opportunities to begin to develop graduate attributes. Recognising the benefit of relevant work-based experience, as part of Ryland's pre-arrival support, he was able to complete a short school-based placement:

> *I have worked with children and young people for years, which was my motivation to train to teach, but I was not able to get school-based experience because of the requirements around Disclosure and Barring Service (DBS) and safeguarding. The course specific aspect of my pre-arrival activity gave me the opportunity to undertake a work-based placement which gave me a real insight into my chosen field of study. The experience opened doors and helped me to get to where I wanted to be. This really helped build my confidence, prepare me for higher education, and laid the groundwork for my future.*

Outcome

Following completion of his pre-entry access support, Ryland successfully completed his teacher education course. Ryland is currently an Assistant Head Teacher in a large secondary age-phase school in England.

Case study 2: Susan

Susan's passion to undertake a new career was ignited by her many years of voluntary work with a charity that supports people in crisis. Susan is a mature student with adult children. Susan held sufficient qualifications to access Higher Education, but as a first-generation higher education student, with no close family to ask about what to expect, coupled with her age, Susan was extremely nervous about returning to study.

How the pre-arrival support helped

In her own words, Susan explains how her institutions getting started at university pre-arrival platform helped her to find her feet and prepare for the academic rigours of university and return to study.

> *I had been out of education for a long time and personal barriers prevented me from undertaking degree level study, which I needed as a first step to get the career I wanted. I didn't know how to move forward but plucked up the courage to attend an open day and have never looked back.*
>
> *Studying in higher education is both the hardest and the most amazing thing I have ever done. I was delighted when I secured my place at university, but then worried about my age and being the only person unable to answer questions. It brought back dreadful memories of my worst school days. I lost confidence and almost reneged on my place. Taking advantage of the pre-arrival support gave me untold confidence. I was extremely*

nervous, but the support I received before starting the course put me at ease. I was encouraged to join a group where I was able to meet current students, and others about to start university. During the group chats it was heartening to discover everyone felt just like me!

The pre-arrival activities helped me to discover how strong I am. I thought I would struggle, but the activities helped me to organise myself. I can do things now that I would never have imagined before. I am a mature lady with children, so I thought I would not fit in, but the student population is diverse. I enjoy being one of the older ones. Often the younger students come to me for guidance, I am like their second mum. The pre-arrival activities made me realise that you are never too old and gave me confidence that has been the catalyst that is changing my life.

The pre-arrival support was excellent. There was a combination of online tasks I could work through on my own at my own pace, recorded sessions I could watch, but I was also able to attend some workshops in real time. One of the tasks explored assessment which helped me to understand the different ways my assignments would be marked. It sounds silly now, but when I started, I did not know the difference between a lecture, seminar, or tutorial. Experiencing them as part of my university preparation, helped me to understand the purpose of each. De-mystifying what I would be walking into helped to alleviate my anxiety, and this helped me to be ready to learn the minute I stepped through the door.

Outcome

Susan is excelling in her studies and is on track to secure a first-class honours degree.

Conclusion

Providing a package of comprehensive support, strategically designed pre-arrival platforms can play a crucial role in supporting the smooth transition of students into higher education. Strategies including academic study skills workshops can be effective in providing targeted support to help students reach their full potential.

Compiled from the strategies discussed in this chapter, features of successful pre-arrival approaches that support non-traditional students in particular include:

1. Orientation: A well-designed platform of pre-arrival induction activity can help build confidence, instil motivation, and equip learners to navigate the nuances of the higher education system.
2. Academic preparation: Activity designed to help learners bridge gaps in their knowledge or skills, strengthening their academic foundation can

give them increased confidence to embark on their higher education journey. Nurturing academic resilience to help learners face challenges or setbacks they may encounter during their time at university is key.

3. Collaboration: Effective pre-arrival support facilitates collaboration with student services helping to ensure that a student's needs are addressed, and targeted support is made available early on in their programme. Signposting to university services at this early stage helps manage pre-arrival nerves, build confidence and in doing so lay solid foundations to support the development of academic resilience (Olson et al., 2022).

4. Supportive communities: An effective pre-arrival curriculum may support students transition via engagement with physical and online groups to help foster a sense of belonging. Mentoring and peer support may also be a feature, where current students help new learners to navigate challenges and begin the adjustment to their new academic life.

5. Communication: Comprehensive, tailored information to help students understand what to expect and feel more prepared for the academic journey ahead is essential. Helping alleviate apprehension, providing clear channels for questions, assistance and ensuring timely support, effective communication is a crucial element of any pre-arrival platform.

Pre-arrival strategies that specifically address the needs and concerns of nontraditional learners can help build a supportive foundation before they begin their higher education journey. Articulated through their voices, students with experience of such initiatives recall how engagement gave them a sense of achievement, increased feelings of esteem and boosted their confidence. By providing information, academic preparation, mentorship, and tailored support, these strategies enhance the likelihood of a successful transition and improve academic outcomes for students.

References

Betts, T., & Oprandi, P. (Eds.). (2022). *Active learning network: 100 ideas for active learning*, University of Sussex Library. https://openpress.sussex.ac.uk/ideasforactivelearning/

Bolton, P. (2023). *Higher education student numbers: Research briefing*. House of Commons Library. Retrieved September 10, 2023, from https://researchbriefings.files.parliament.uk/documents/CBP-7857/CBP-7857.pdf.

Bolton, P., & Lewis, J. (2023). *Equality of access and outcomes in higher education in England*. Research Briefing. House of Commons Library. Retrieved September 11, 2023, from https://researchbriefings.files.parliament.uk/documents/CBP-9195/CBP-9195.pdf.

British Council. (2020). *FIRST STEPS: A pre-departure guide for international students coming to study in the UK, 2019–2020*. Retrieved September 10,

2023, from www.britishcouncil.org/sites/default/files/k071_01_studyuk_first_steps_a5_final_web.pdf.

Chernikova, O., Heitzmann, N., Stadler, M., Holzberger, D., Seidel, T., & Fischer, F. (2020). Simulation-based learning in higher education: A meta-analysis. *Review of Educational Research, 90*(4), 499–541. https://journals.sagepub.com/doi/pdf/10.3102/0034654320933544

Finch, J. (1987). The vignette technique in survey research. *Sociology, 21*(2), 105–114.

Gray, D., Royall, B., & Malson, H. (2017). Hypothetically speaking: Using vignettes as a stand-alone qualitative method. In V. Braun, V. Clarke, & D. Gray (Eds.), *Collecting qualitative data: A practical guide to textual, media and virtual techniques*. Cambridge University Press. https://uwe-repository.worktribe.com/output/835120

Hubble, S., & Bolton, P. (2021). *Mature higher education students in England.* Briefing Paper 8809. House of Commons library. Retrieved July 6, 2023, from https://commonslibrary.parliament.uk/research-briefings/cbp-8809/.

Irving-Bell, D. (2019). *How to design a research poster.* The National Teaching Repository. Poster. https://doi.org/10.25416/edgehill.10563953

Irving-Bell, D., & Hartley, P. (2022). Visual thinking: Exploring current practices and perspectives re student notetaking. *Journal of Learning Development in Higher Education*, (25). https://journal.aldinhe.ac.uk/index.php/jldhe/article/view/963

Office for Students. (2021). *Improving opportunity and choice for mature students.* Retrieved September 11, 2023, from www.officeforstudents.org.uk/publications/improving-opportunity-and-choice-for-mature-students/.

Olson, C., Briscoe, H., & Prior, M. (2022). *Grow your academic resilience!* [Poster presentation]. The National Teaching Repository. https://doi.org/10.25416/NTR.20156927

Sampson, H., & Johannessen, I. A. (2020). Turning on the tap: The benefits of using 'real-life' vignettes in qualitative research interviews. *Qualitative Research, 20*(1), 56–72.

UCAS. (2023). *Mature undergraduate students.* Retrieved September 10, 2023, from www.ucas.com/undergraduate/applying-university/mature-undergraduate-students#:~:text=Typically%2C%20this%20will%20mean%20students,around%2040%25%20are%20over%2030.

12 Using pre-arrival platforms to support postgraduate students' transition

Adam Paxman

Part of Edge Hill University's (EHU) Library and Learning Services department, the Student Engagement Team (SET) provides academic writing and information skills support for students on Access to Higher Education, undergraduate (UG) and postgraduate taught (PGT) programmes. The support service is branded UniSkills. Here, we discuss pre-arrival induction and transition online resources with a particular focus on the Transition into Postgraduate Study webinar, first delivered in summer 2022. We draw on an institutional PGT Student Experience Developmental Enquiry Report (2019), sources synthesised from a literature review by Jamieson (2019) and additional secondary research. Session design considerations are explored, allowing for reflections on pedagogy, efficacy and improvements. As such, this chapter touches on several key themes from this book: session development; engendering belonging; and diverse student populations.

A gap in research?

A literature review by Helen Jamieson (2019), the Head of Student Engagement at EHU, acknowledged that there is 'significantly less research' on PGT student experience than on UG student experience or indeed induction and transition, with 'PGT occupying an ambiguous space between undergraduate and research pathways' (McPherson et al., 2017; Poon, 2019; Morgan, 2014b; Tobbell et al., 2010; Bownes et al., 2017; Hallett, 2010, and Bamber et al., 2019). This is despite large scale analyses of Postgraduate Taught Experience Survey (PTES) data by authors such as Poon (2019) and Muijs and Bokhove (2017). Adding to this identified gap, there is a dearth of sources on PGT student experience, induction and transition specific to the period of rapid wholesale migration of teaching, learning and assessment to an online context which resulted from the worldwide COVID pandemic and consequent national lockdowns. Leman (2021) proves an exception, based on PTES data. The case study described here was developed based on what research is available pertaining to postgraduate students.

DOI: 10.4324/9781003427575-16

A case study of postgraduate pre-arrival platforms

Institutional context

Over 70% of EHU students possess at least one Widening Participation (WP) characteristic (Edge Hill University, 2019). A post-1992 university originally founded as the country's first non-denominational teaching college for women, EHU is located in the Northwest of England, and support for disadvantaged students is 'an integral element' of the institution and its resource allocation (Edge Hill University, 2017, p. 1).

A Postgraduate Taught Student Experience Developmental Enquiry (2019) reported that as of 2018–2019, there were over six times more part-time than full-time PGT students at EHU. This excluded those individuals studying Postgraduate Certificate in Education (PGCE) programmes. The PGT demographic at EHU was identified as ethnically White by a significant majority, with most Black, Asian and Minority Ethnic (BAME) – or rather Global Ethnic Majority (GEM) (Loy, 2023) – PGT students studying professional qualifications in the Faculty of Education or the Faculty of Health, Social Care and Medicine. PGT students were twice as likely to be female than male, over 25 and from the Northwest region. Student feedback corroborated that PGT students are likely to lead complex lives with multiple responsibilities outside their studies, including challenges with travel, childcare, employment and caring responsibilities. This institutional diversity and the need for higher education institutions (HEIs) to be mindful of the consequent academic, personal and pastoral needs of PGT students are identified by O'Donnell et al. (2009), Tobbell, O'Donnell and Zammit (2010) and Morgan (2014a).

Development of the pre-arrival webinar

Transition into PGT Study, a pre-arrival webinar is co-presented by two academic skills advisors (ASAs), so as to engender rapport and trust. Students are encouraged to interact with presenters and to ask questions throughout the session via BlackBoard Collaborate's chat function. The first slide, which is on display before the webinar, explains how to access the chat function.

Link to research

As O'Donnell et al. (2009) noted, PGT students can struggle with changes in technology and learning technology that have occurred during variable gaps in education and be unprepared for a shift to more blended and interactive teaching, learning and assessment strategies. Although Evans et al. (2018) note PGT students are aware study at this level will be different to prior learning experiences, McPherson et al. (2017) suggest the importance of a clear definition and management of expectations of PGT study. Jamieson (2019) establishes consensus between McPherson et al. (2017) and Bamber et al. (2019) that PGT level work:

> centres around autonomy, self-assessment, self-regulation, self-management, more intellectually demanding material, considerably less direction from staff and increased [. . .] criticality.

This supports the need for a rigorous support framework, as suggested by Coneyworth et al. (2019).

The tone of the webinar is intended to be welcoming and reassuring, as according to Broadhead et al.(2019), Broadhead and Garland (2012), Kane et al. (2014) and Reay (2004), self-doubt, imposter syndrome and lack of confidence are likely to be experienced by PGT and UG students alike. According to Tobbell et al. (2010), McPherson et al. (2017) and Bownes et al. (2017), contrary to conventional assumptions, PGT students are not shielded from the transition to Level 7 study by previous academic experiences. They may struggle with feeling like novices or experience anxiety after having mastered undergraduate study – often in a discrete discipline. In accordance with O'Donnell et al. (2009) and Patel (2019), academic skills advisors acknowledge the diversity and complexity of PGT students' lives.

Self-reflection

A Padlet activity provides an opportunity to self-reflect on prior learning, with prompts on academic skills developed through UG study, employment or otherwise. Students are also encouraged to describe their feelings about PGT study, affording ASAs opportunities to build students' confidence, offer reassurance, manage expectations and discuss imposter syndrome, signposting to other Getting Started with UniSkills pre-arrival webinars, resources and/or support services as appropriate.

Link to research

The importance of establishing and supporting underpinning academic skills is highlighted by several studies, including but not limited to O'Donnell et al. (2009), McPherson et al. (2017), and Bamber et al. (2019). The significance of self-reflection in supporting a diverse PGT cohort is highlighted by Morgan (2015) and Liu and Pullinger (2021).

Induction framework

Although Morgan (2023) recommends that successful induction and transition activities should bridge academic and social information, Getting Started with UniSkills focuses on academic skills. This is due to the nature of SET as a service and its generic – meaning non-subject-specific – position within the institution. Faculty-based, subject-specific induction activities also take place for all programmes, supplemented by additional pastoral induction information from other support services.

Link to research

One improvement that came about as a direct result of the EHU developmental enquiry in 2018–2019 was the establishment of a standardised Student Induction Framework – something highlighted as essential by Morgan (2015) to counter gaps in PGT pre-entry transition and induction activities which can occur due to the assumption of the PGT student as already expert (O'Donnell et al., 2009; Tobbell et al., 2010; McPherson et al., 2017). Liu and Pullinger (2021) identify information literacy and academic skills as PGT induction foci within the Step Up to Masters programme at University of Leeds, an award winning programme.

Recapitulating foundational academic skills

Raising awareness of other potential barriers to learning for PGT students, guidance is provided within the Transitioning into PGT Study webinar on transitioning to Level 7, outlining some of the peculiar challenges identified by the Postgraduate Taught Experience Survey 2015 (Advance HE, 2016) and discussed by Leman (2015). These include but are not limited to increased workload, pace and independent learning. To combat common barriers identified by Barnes et al. (2018), and to build upon foundational academic skills, webinar content includes guidance on and opportunities to discuss academic reading and writing skills, finding academic information and criticality.

Link to research

PGT survey data examined by Neves and Leman (2019) and Leman (2020), as well as literature reviews by Liu and Pullinger (2021) and Jamieson (2019) support the importance of including these key academic skills.

Support systems and learning communities

In the webinar, students are encouraged to join a learning community, either by seeking out subject-based groups in their faculties, or by engaging with UniSkills' regular UG and PGT in-person workshop Returning to Learning (R2L). At the end of the webinar, ASAs signpost students to UniSkills in-person workshops and webinars, in-person or online 1–2–1 appointments and online resources, thereby empowering them as individuals to access relevant support as required.

Link to research

Robust and accessible student support systems are considered as important as course delivery by Hallett (2010) and Jancey and Burns (2013), while Bownes et al. (2017) identify a supportive peer community as significant to supporting transition and easing anxiety. Empowering students to access support is in line with findings by Jamieson (2019) and Liu and Pullinger (2021). As opposed to an initial or short-term induction intervention, the sustained 'acculturation of students into new educational spaces' (Jones et al., 2020) and learning communities through a long-term model of induction and transition is identified by both Biesta (2010) and Patel (2019) as a key facet of engendering a positive educational experience. Bamber et al. (2019) and Evans et al. (2018) support the need for a longer-term induction model, based upon both the short-term nature of many PGT programmes, and the intensiveness of Level 7 study.

Longer-term induction in practice

The webinar and bespoke PGT applicants' webpage are supplemented by three additional UG/PGT Getting Started with UniSkills pre-arrival webinars on academic writing, research skills and academic resilience. Although several sources identified by Jamieson (2019) support the view that PGT students prefer resources specific to them, delivery of the webinars for separate UG and PGT cohorts was deemed impractical. Notwithstanding this, an expanded version of the Transition into PGT Study session is available in face-to-face workshop and online synchronous delivery modes at regular intervals throughout the academic year, as part of the UniSkills workshop programme. Regular R2L community meetings support a model of induction which is not solely focused on pre-arrival activities. Such a model was recommended as best practice by the 2018–2019 Postgraduate Student Experience Developmental Enquiry.

PGT students' heterogeneous lives and curvilinear paths

SET developed the PGT-specific pre-arrival webinar and tailored PGT applicants' webpages and learning community as direct results of the 2019 developmental enquiry report. Additionally, an institutional Student Induction Framework (2019) was developed to address priorities and challenges identified by students during focus groups. This included recommendations for standardised Learning and Support Services online induction sessions and also induction webpages, online wiki guides and applicants' webpages, highlighting the positive impact of staff–student co-creation.

Link to research

Broadhead et al. (2019, p. 139) state

> non-traditional and mature students do not have linear learning journeys where levels of learning are incremental.

Panel meetings, student focus groups and a literature review conducted by Jamieson (2019), consistently supported the importance of PGT induction, learning communities to promote belonging, and the use of language and resources tailored specifically to PGT students. The importance of the latter was identified by Humphrey and McCarthy (1999).

Session design and guiding principles

Academic skills, metacognition to critically reflect on learning and barriers were all incorporated into the session content. The webinar was designed as an interactive, discursive opportunity, signposting PGT students to R2L and faculty learning communities.

Link to research

Tasked with the creation of the Transitioning into PGT Study pre-arrival webinar, the UK Quality Code HE qualification frameworks (QAA, 2014), Association of Learning Developers in Higher Education (ALDinHE) values and research by Wilkinson (2005) and Hounsell et al. (2008) were used to shape the session design. The correlation between Wilkinson's (2005, p. 10) description of postgraduate 'learning journeys' which are seldom a 'methodical and clearly structured path' and Patel's (2019) recognition of the idiosyncrasies of PGT student experience, as well as the acknowledgement of O'Donnell et al. (2009) of the heterogeneity of PG students, is clear. Wilkinson (2005, p. 10) identifies a focus on 'self-management', 'basic' academic skills and culture and PGT students' metacognition to critically reflect on learning as important. O'Donnell et al. (2009) also highlight academic skills and practices, as well as a gap in education, as significant barriers to learning for PGT students. Hounsell et al. (2008) underscore the importance of peers in improving understanding and providing support.

Reflection and further development

A move to an interactive toolkit

Initially, there was poor uptake of the expanded on-programme version, and it was suggested that this in-person workshop and webinar content could be more beneficial for students if reworked as an interactive toolkit. That way, PGT students would be able to access the resource as and when required from the UniSkills webpages. This type of selection and access was commented upon favourably by O'Donnell et al. (2009), Jamieson (2019) and Liu and Pullinger (2021).

Bespoke PGT applicants' webpage

Amendments to the tone of voice used on EHU applicants' webpage led to the creation of a separate, bespoke PGT applicants' webpage. The new webpage was subsequently flagged at the interdepartmental Welcome Communications Group, so that PGT students would receive a PGT-specific pre-arrival email signposting them to the bespoke webpage and webinar.

Student feedback mechanisms

The recent establishment of several student advisory panels at EHU will provide future opportunities for detailed student feedback on both the UG and PGT pre-arrival webinars, as well as the applicants' webpages and accompanying resources. This will be in addition to guidance from the initial student focus groups which formed part of the 2018–2019 developmental enquiry, as well as feedback from Student Advisors working with SET frequently throughout the academic year.

Conclusions

The literature is consistent in many regards as to what constitutes effective induction support for PGT students. A clear definition of PGT study is essential. The frequent acknowledgement of PGT population diversity and complexity is desirable. Self-reflection, self-management and foundational academic skills should not be assumed but rather scaffolded. Resources and communications specific to PGT students are desirable. A long-term induction and transition model is efficacious, given the intensive nature and short duration of many PGT programmes. Induction support which scaffolds information literacies is also desirable, as rapid changes in technology during variable gaps in education can otherwise become significant barriers to learning. Peer communities are desirable to provide additional academic, social and pastoral support, as well as to engender belonging and to diminish anxiety and imposter syndrome. A robust institutional induction framework is also desirable.

References

AdvanceHE.(2016).*Postgraduatetaughtexperiencesurvey2015*.www.advance-he.ac.uk/knowledge-hub/postgraduate-taught-experience-survey-2015

Bamber, V., Choudhary, C. J., Hislop, J., & Lane, J. (2019). Postgraduate taught students and preparedness for master's level study: Polishing the facets of the master's diamond. *Journal of Further and Higher Education, 43*(2), 236–250. https://doi.org/10.1080/0309877X.2017.1359502

Barnes, T., Macleod, G., & Huttly, S. R. A. (2018). *National survey of PGT programme directors and administrators.* UK Council for Graduate Education. https://ukcge.ac.uk/assets/resources/29-National-Survey-of-PGT-Directors-and-Administrators-2018.pdf

Biesta, G. J. (2010). *Good education in an age of measurement: Ethics, politics, democracy.* Paradigm Publishers.

Bownes, J., Labrosse, N., Forrest, D., MacTaggart, D., Senn, H., Fischbacher-Smith, M., & Biletskaya, T. (2017). Supporting students in the transition to postgraduate taught study in stem subjects. *Journal of Perspectives in Applied Academic Practice, 5*(2), 3–11. https://doi.org/10.14297/jpaap.v5i2.280

Broadhead, S., Davies, R., & Hudson, A. (2019). *Perspectives on access to higher education: Practice and research.* Emerald Group Publishing.

Broadhead, S., & Garland, S. (2012). *The art of surviving and thriving: How well are access students prepared for their degrees in art and design?* University of Brighton. http://arts.brighton.ac.uk/projects/networks/issue-17-april-2012/the-art-of-surviving-and-thriving-how-well-are-access-students-prepared-for-their-degrees-in-art-and-design

Coneyworth, L., Jessop, R., Maden, P., & White, G. (2019). The overlooked cohort? Improving the taught postgraduate student experience in higher education. *Innovations in Education and Teaching International, 57*(3), 262–273. https://doi.org/10.1080/14703297.2019.1617184

Edge Hill University. (2017). *Edge Hill University access agreement 2018–2019.* www.edgehill.ac.uk/wp-content/uploads/documents/access-agreement-2018-2019.pdf

Edge Hill University. (2019). *Access and participation plan 2020/21–2024/25.* www.edgehill.ac.uk/document/access-participation-plan/

Evans, C., Nguyen, T., Richardson, M., & Scott, I. (2018). Managing the transition from undergraduate to taught postgraduate study: Perceptions of international students studying in the UK. *Research in Post-compulsory Education, 23*(2), 249–265. https://doi.org/10.1080/13596748.2018.1444386

Hallett, F. (2010). The postgraduate student experience of study support: A phenomenographic analysis. *Studies in Higher Education, 35*(2), 225–238. https://doi.org/10.1080/03075070903134234

Hounsell, J., Christie, H., Cree, V., McCune, V., & Tett, L. (2008). Talking and sharing: The role of peer support and retention in higher education. *Journal of Access, Policy and Practice, 6*(1), 35–51.

Humphrey, R., & McCarthy, P. (1999). Recognising difference: Providing for postgraduate students. *Studies in Higher Education, 24*(3), 371–386. https://doi.org/10.1080/03075079912331379955

Jamieson, H. (2019). Literature review. In *Developmental enquiry: The postgraduate taught student experience report, June 2019.* [in-house publication] (pp. 66–73). Edge Hill University.

Jancey, J., & Burns, S. (2013). Institutional factors and the postgraduate student experience. *Quality Assurance in Education, 21,* 311–322. https://doi.org/10.1108/QAE-Nov-2011-0069

Jones, A., Olds, A., & Lisciandro, J. G. (2020). Transitioning students into higher education. In *Philosophy, pedagogy and practice.* Routledge.

Kane, S., Chalcraft, D., & Volpe, G. (2014). Notions of belonging: First year, first semester higher education students enrolled on business or economics degree programmes. *The International Journal of Management Education, 12*(2), 193–201. https://doi.org/10.1016/j.ijme.2014.04.001

Leman, J. (2015). What do taught postgraduates want? In *The postgraduate taught experience survey.* Higher Education Academy. https://s3.eu-west-2.amazonaws.com/assets.creode.advancehe-document-manager/documents/hea/private/ptes_2015_what_do_pgts_want_1568037339.pdf

Leman, J. (2020). *Postgraduate taught experience survey 2020.* Advance HE. www.advance-he.ac.uk/knowledge-hub/postgraduate-taught-experience-survey-2020

Leman, J. (2021). *Global pandemic not over for taught postgraduate students.* Advance HE. www.advance-he.ac.uk/news-and-views/global-pandemic-not-over-taught-postgraduate-students

Liu, J., & Pullinger, D. (2021). Step up to masters: Supporting the academic skills transition for taught postgraduate students. *Journal of Information Literacy, 15*(3), 100–118. http://dx.doi.org/10.11645/15.3.3095

Loy, R. (2023). *Why we're no longer using BAME.* National Museums Liverpool. Why we're no longer using BAME | National Museums Liverpool (liverpoolmuseums.org.uk)

McPherson, C., Punch, S., & Graham, E. A. (2017). Transitions from undergraduate to taught postgraduate study: Emotion, integration and ambiguity. *Journal of Perspectives in Applied Academic Practice, 5*(2), 42–50. https://doi.org/10.14297/jpaap.v5i2.265

Morgan, M. (2014a). Study expectations of 1st/2nd generation STEM postgraduate taught students. *Quality Assurance in Education, 22*(2), 169–184. https://doi.org/10.1108/QAE-03-2013-0014

Morgan, M. (2014b). Patterns, drivers and challenges pertaining to postgraduate taught study: An international comparative analysis. *Higher Education Research & Development, 33*(6), 1150–1165. https://doi.org/10.1080/0729 4360.2014.911258

Morgan, M. (2015). Study expectations of different domiciled postgraduate-taught students in a UK post-1992-institution. *Quality Assurance in Education, 23*(3), 233–249. https://doi.org/10.1108/QAE-02-2014-0005

Morgan, M. (2023). *Improving the student experience in higher education: Support and advice for staff.* www.improvingthestudentexperience.com/

Muijs, D., & Bokhove, C. (2017). Postgraduate student satisfaction: A multilevel analysis of PTES data. *British Educational Research Journal, 43*(5), 904–930. https://doi.org/10.1002/berj.3294

Neves, J., & Leman, J. (2019). *2019 postgraduate taught experience survey*. Advance HE. https://s3.eu-west-2.amazonaws.com/assets. creode.advancehe-document-manager/documents/advance-he/PTES-2019_1573558819.pdf

O'Donnell, V. L., Tobbell, J., Lawthom, R., & Zammit, M. (2009). Transition to postgraduate study: Practice, participation and the widening participation agenda. *Active Learning in Higher Education, 10*(1), 26–40. https://doi.org/10.1177/1469787408100193

Patel, A. (2019). *Supporting transition to and during postgraduate study*. University of Birmingham. www.birmingham.ac.uk/news-archive/2019/supporting-transition-to-and-during-postgraduate-study

Poon, J. (2019). Postgraduate student satisfaction in the UK. *Property Management, 37*(1), 115–135. https://doi.org/10.1108/PM-07-2017-0041

Quality Assurance Agency. (2014). *UK quality code for higher education. Part A: Setting and maintaining academic standards*. The Frameworks for Higher Education Qualifications of UK Degree-Awarding Bodies. QAA. www.qaa.ac.uk/docs/qaa/quality-code/qualifications-frameworks.pdf

Reay, D. (2004). Finding or losing yourself. In *The RoutledgeFalmer reader in the sociology of education* (pp. 30–44). RoutledgeFalmer.

Tobbell, J., O'Donnell, V., & Zammit, M. (2010). Exploring transition to postgraduate study: Shifting identities in interaction with communities, practice and participation. *British Educational Research Journal, 36*(2), 261–278. https://doi.org/10.1080/01411920902836360

Wilkinson, D. (2005). *The essential guide to postgraduate study*. SAGE Publications, Limited.

13 Enhancing student transition to university

Innovative pre-arrival platforms through a connective ecosystem

Kathy Egea, Katie Padilla, Jason Do, Deanna Horvath and Christopher Bridge

The Australian Higher Education Standards Framework (Australian Government, 2021), states in addressing the minimum standards for student transition into university 'Students should have equivalent opportunities for successful transition and progression . . . irrespective of their educational background, entry pathway, mode or place of study' (Section.1.3.6). However, recent research in Australia (Harris-Reeves et al., 2022) reveals that a considerable number of commencing students feel inadequately prepared for academic life, resulting in a notable lack of retention. To succeed, students must navigate and negotiate the educational interface (Kahu & Nelson, 2018) to develop self-efficacy, a sense of belonging, and overall well-being.

One significant challenge lies in the fragmented and siloed approach between curricular and co-curricular strategies to student transition, including in the pre-arrival stage. The diverse and robust practice underpinning pre-arrival platforms presents an exceptional opportunity for academics and professional staff to share practice towards seamless student transition and build a connective ecosystem.

To address the need for a smoother transition, purposeful pre-arrival programmes play a vital role. In this context, we present three case studies from two Australian universities focussing on pre-arrival platforms designed to promote successful transitioning in various contexts, encompassing overall university study, faculty integration and subject-specific adjustments. These selected practices cater to diverse student cohorts, including international and equity-disadvantaged backgrounds.

Each case study delves into the design, implementation, and the resulting impact of the pre-arrival programmes on students' transition into university or engagement in their studies, highlighting practices that nurture student identity, capacity, confidence, academic and university culture, a sense of belonging and peer friendships.

We conclude by identifying transferable practices derived from the case studies, applicable in both curriculum and co-curriculum domains.

DOI: 10.4324/9781003427575-17

Establishing collaborative partnerships between academics and those who support students outside the classroom, as suggested by Kift (2015), not only provides new ways to support the widening diversity of current cohorts but also fosters the development of a connective ecosystem and more cohesive and wholistic approach towards student transition.

Case study 1: University approach: pre-arrival platform for international students

The University of Technology Sydney (UTS) welcomes approximately 1,200 incoming exchange and study abroad students annually from various regions including Europe, North and South America, for one or two semesters. To support these students in this challenge, and to give them a sense of student identity, sense of belonging to UTS, and understandings of intercultural learning within the Australian culture, the pre-arrival online platform called Culture Connect was designed and implemented in 2021 (Spring session) using UTS Learning Management System (LMS) online platform, providing students with 24/7 access.

Culture Connect aimed to create safe and welcoming spaces for students to share experiences, thoughts, ideas, fears and commonalities. Drawing from First and Further Year Experience Programme practices (see Egea, 2022) that introduced staff to the concepts of humanising the online curriculum, pedagogies of care and compassion, practices in belonging and wellness, and having fun, while at the same time addressing university strategies for personalised learning, the online platform went beyond information about university life and became a rich supportive platform mapped to the student learning journey (see Figure 13.1). Students consider joining UTS at least six months prior to

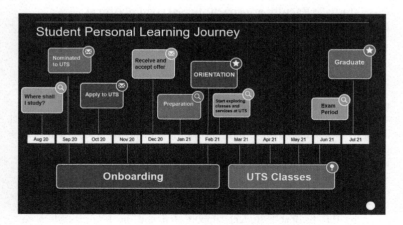

Figure 13.1 Map of Student Personal Learning Journey (Study Abroad Programme)

enrolling at the university. Students are encouraged to enrol in Culture Connect as soon as they are accepted by the university, while still in their home country. Modules are adaptively released, to provide 'just *in time*' administrative support, videos on indigenous and intercultural learning about Australia and links to student support and counselling.

The modules use friendly and accessible language, and include interactive elements such as announcements, videos (with captions), quizzes, social polls and community discussion boards. Through these interactive elements, Culture Connect promotes student connection and capacity building by encouraging students to engage with one another and to reflect on their experiences.

Students engage early with the Culture Connect program, as seen in the 2023 LMS analytics, with almost 19,000 page views made by 473 enrolled students for Module 2 (*Your gateway to Australia*) when released in the first week of January 2023. Students' feedback indicated that 90% of students enjoyed the whole program, what it has taught them and how it has supported and connected them to UTS (programmes, infrastructure and fellow students) and Australian culture.

Culture Connect continues to be a valuable tool to support incoming exchange and study abroad students, with adaptations being explored to cater further for the in-person and on-campus experience. The designers reflect that using the UTS LMS as soon as students are admitted into the university was useful to familiarise students with the online platform prior to study, and that it was suitable for both onshore and offshore student cohorts. They continue to improve the program, such as embedding Portfolium (software tool for career development) so that students can showcase their skills from their learning.

Case study 2: Faculty approach: pre-arrival platform for international students

The Faculty of Engineering and Information Technology (FEIT), at UTS, has implemented a co-design 'students as partners' approach to assist international students in their transition into and through university. The programmes were designed to address the transitional needs of international students, prior to students arriving on campus.

International students applied for the paid role of i-Ambassadors and were engaged to conduct surveys and interviews with undergraduate and postgraduate international students. Their findings identified several transitional issues faced by international students and include differences in educational systems, culture shock, social isolation, homesickness, communication, financial arrangements and career support. These issues are reflected in Australian literature (see Newton et al., 2021).

Using this feedback, student support staff and the I-Ambassadors co-designed three key initiatives. The first was the FEIT Survival Guide, an

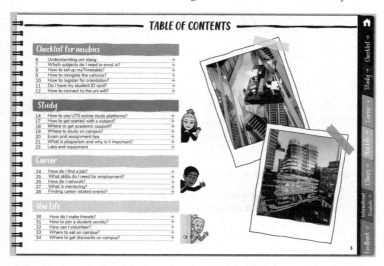

Figure 13.2 Table of Contents from 2023 UTS FEIT Survival Guide

interactive online guide that is accessible not only to international students but for all FEIT students. The Survival Guide is organised into five categories: Getting Started, Study, Careers, Uni Life, and with special sections for international students (see Figure 13.2 for content pages in Survival Guide). It has been well-received by students and has helped them adjust to university life during their first semester of study. Other faculties have also expressed interest in adapting the Survival Guide to their context, as well as used for within the university-wide orientation program.

The second initiative is the i-Mentor program, which focuses on creating student connections before students arrive on campus. Student mentors, including domestic and international students, were recruited and trained to build relationships with small groups of commencing students. These mentors act as a bridge for their engagement with the wider landscape of the faculty and the university.

The third initiative is the i-Support Program, designed to support offshore students' sense of belonging and social connection. The programme draws from the FEIT Survival Guide and i-Mentor programme and includes academic support through an online platform with chunked modules and self-tests on active learning, classroom expectations, assessment styles, plagiarism and UTS Support (Figure 13.3). Additionally, it offers well-being and return to campus support through peer-to-peer mentoring, social media (WeChat) for the offshore Chinese student community, and a culture of increased openness and peer support.

Figure 13.3 UTS i-Support Program

FEIT's student-centred approach to supporting international students' transitions has been successful, with the initiatives improving the overall transition experience for international students, beyond the faculty. The pre-arrival online platforms, including the mentor program, are particularly helpful in supporting international students before they arrive on campus, giving them a head start in adjusting to their new environment. These student-partner initiatives continue to promote a culture of collaborative learning, social connection and peer support, while also providing access to student support services.

Case study 3: Subject-based: pre-arrival platform for diverse cohorts

The Get Ready Programme is a set of short pre-arrival online transition programmes aimed at enhancing the sense of belonging among students, particularly for equity groups who typically perceive greater 'social incongruence' than traditional student cohorts with respect to the academic community they are entering (Devlin & McKay, 2014). Targeted equity groups consist of students who are first-in-family, from a low socioeconomic background, and/or with a low tertiary admission rank. The programme serves a wide range of health and science degree programmes, encompassing very large first-year science subjects, at La Trobe's multi-campus university. Students have both domestic and international backgrounds.

Upon enrolment into their subjects, students receive an invitation to participate in the program, and detailed instructions are provided on how to use the La Trobe LMS. The programme starts with a diagnostic quiz. As many students, not just those from equity groups, experience anxiety at the prospect of taking a first-year science subject, in particular those who have previously

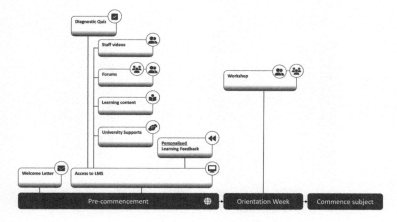

Figure 13.4 Timeline of Get Ready: Stages of transition support

studied little or no biology or chemistry, or who have not studied for a number of years, the diagnostic test has high participation rates. Students who score under 80% in the quiz are recommended to participate in the program. The pre-arrival programme is open to all students to avoid stigmatising those who take part (Larsen et al., 2020).

The Get Ready Program's LMS introduces students to key concepts and terminology for the early weeks of the subject, focusing on areas of difficulty. Students can self-test to check their understanding. There are short explanatory videos presented by the academics in a warm and encouraging manner. Students are encouraged to join the carefully monitored discussion forums to interact with their peers and teaching staff. Students are recommended to purchase the online text, prompted towards help-seeking behaviour, encouraged to share questions in the online forum and act as a resource to support each other's learning. At the final stage of Get Ready, students are invited to an on-campus orientation week workshop. The workshop is enacted in the classroom, and students work with peers in group activities to revise the learning material, and teaching staff are available to problem-solve. Figure 13.4 presents the timeline of this program, highlighting the stages of transition support.

Each component of the programme is carefully designed to address Lizzio's Five Senses Model (Lizzio, 2006), a practical framework specifically intended to guide the design of transition programmes. The model highlights the importance of affective elements in making the transition to university study, which enable and foster identification as a novice member of a new learning community. Lizzio's framework categorises these affective elements under five 'senses': those of capacity, resourcefulness, purpose, connection and academic culture. Each of these must be addressed for a transition programme to be effective.

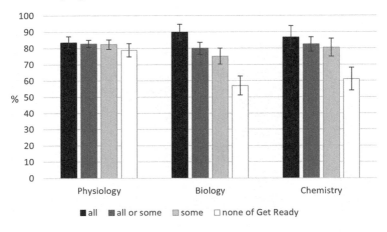

Figure 13.5 Pass rate (%) for equity cohorts according to participation in the Get Ready LMS, with 95% confidence intervals (Larsen et al., 2021, Figure 13.4, p. 10, reprinted with permission).

In Get Ready, students build a sense of capacity in engaging with the LMS, undertaking the weekly low-stakes content and self-evaluating their learning. Their sense of resourcefulness is enabled through understanding how to work with peers and source information, their sense of purpose aligns with their enhanced sense of belonging, their sense of connection with peers and teachers in both the online and workshop activities and a sense of familiarity with the content that they might otherwise find overwhelming (academic culture).

Significantly, Get Ready provides students with low-stakes activities as they learn to use the LMS, adapt to the learning environment in the classroom and acknowledge how peers are part of the learning process. This approach has been shown to improve confidence, pass rates (see Figure 13.5), and retention of equity groups in content-heavy subjects. The programme provides an example of how targeted online transition programmes can support the engagement and success of students from equity groups in large, diverse university settings.

Transferable practices

Kift et al. (2010) and later Kift (2015) argue that programmes, such as pre-arrival programmes, that support student transition into first year need to go beyond silos in faculties and across student support domains: rather '*everyone needs to be at the table*'. To achieve this, they suggest that these separate entities build relationships and share knowledge. With this in mind, this chapter draws out pre-arrival transition practices that not only support the diverse cohorts at both curricular and co-curricular student support, but they also provide an opportunity for new ways of working.

* Cultural Connect was based on the student learning journey, and this could easily move into subject level. Pacansky-Brock et al. (2020) provide practice examples to humanise the curriculum with an understanding of student needs and this learning journey.
* The Survival Guide is a model that students have designed for students both as practice guidance along with the mentor program, engages students at the pre-arrival stage and is found to build belonging, connection and better understanding of academic culture. This could be shared with the student support domain, enacted prior to students arriving on campus for the welcome and orientation program. At UTS, there is some movement in this way, with FEIT i-Mentors modelling best practice.
* Get Ready prepares students for using the LMS, brings in context, culture and connection – a programme to support students to become engaged and confident learners. The programme supplements the longer-term bridging or foundational year and is subject specific. The design of this programme could easily be transferred across a range of first-year subjects that students find difficult, with Lizzio's five senses of success being implemented into the student support domain.

Connecting the dots is critical to build a connective ecosystem to support students in their transition to university: it is the intersection of academic and student support practices to facilitate successful student transition to university. All case studies are designed intentionally to build a positive sense of belonging at university, and this affects students' retention, motivation and enjoyment (Pedler et al., 2022). It is these first encounters that matter (Nelson et al., 2018). At its heart, pre-arrival programmes give students early understandings of the education interface (Kahu & Nelson, 2018) and the practices needed for students to build their own successful transition.

The case studies highlight the critical roles collaborations and partnerships play in enhancing innovative practices in student transition. Having a robust connected ecosystem enables universities to respond to emerging student needs proactively.

References

Australian Government. (2021). *Higher education standards framework (threshold standards)*. Department of Education, Skills and Employment. www.legislation.gov.au/Details/F2022C00105

Devlin, M., & McKay, J. (2014). Reframing 'the problem': Students from low socio-economic status backgrounds transitioning to university. In H. Brook, D. Fergie, M. Maeorg, & D. Michell (Eds.), *Universities in transition: Foregrounding social contexts of knowledge in the first year experience* (pp. 97–125). Adelaide University Press. https://library.oapen. org/bitstream/handle/20.500.12657/33147/560371.pdf

Egea, K (2022). *The FFYE program: Enhancing inclusion with a community of transition practice* [Blog]. Advancing Practice in Academic Development, SEDA. https://thesedablog.wordpress.com/2022/02/24/the-ffye-program/

Harris-Reeves, B., Pearson, A., & Massa, H. (2022). Exploring the expectations and experiences of first year students undergoing a tailored transition initiative. *Journal of University Teaching & Learning Practice, 19*(3). https://ro.uow.edu.au/jutlp/vol19/iss3/16

Kahu, E. R., & Nelson, K. (2018). Student engagement in the educational interface: Understanding the mechanisms of student success. *Higher Education Research and Development, 37*(1), 58–71. https://doi.org/10.1080/0 7294360.2017.1344197

Kift, S. (2015). A decade of transition pedagogy: A quantum leap in conceptualising the first year experience. *HERDA Review of Higher Education, 2*, 51–86.

Kift, S. M., Nelson, K. J., & Clarke, J. A. (2010). Transition pedagogy: A third generation approach to FYE: A case study of policy and practice for the higher education sector. *The International Journal of the First Year in Higher Education, 1*(1), 1–20.

Larsen, A., Cox, S., Bridge, C., Horvath, D., Emmerling, M., & Abrahams, C. (2021). Short, multi-modal, pre-commencement transition programs for a diverse STEM cohort. *Journal of University Teaching & Learning Practice, 18*(3). https://doi.org/10.53761/1.18.3.5

Larsen, A., Horvath, D., & Bridge, C. (2020). 'Get ready': Improving the transition experience of a diverse first year cohort through building student agency. *Student Success, 11*(2), 14–27. https://doi.org/10.5204/ssj.v11i3.1144

Lizzio, A. (2006). *Designing an orientation and transition strategy for commencing students: A conceptual summary of research and practice.* First year experience project. Griffith University.

Nelson, K., Readman, K., & Stoodley, I. (2018). *Shaping the 21st century student experience at regional universities.* Final report. https://research. usq.edu.au/item/q75x9/shaping-the-21st-century-student-experience-at-regional-universities-final-report

Newton, D. C., LaMontagne, A., & Tomyn, A. (2021). Exploring the challenges and opportunities for improving the health and wellbeing of international students: Perspectives of professional staff at an Australian University. *Journal of the Australian and New Zealand Student Services Association, 29*(1),74–92.

Pacansky-Brock, M., Smedshammer, M., & Vincent-Layton, K. (2020). Humanizing online teaching to equitize higher education. *Current Issues in Education, 21*(2).

Pedler, M. L., Willis, R., & Nieuwoudt, J. E. (2022). A sense of belonging at university: Student retention, motivation and enjoyment. *Journal of Further and Higher Education, 46*(3), 397–408. https://doi.org/10.1080/0309 877X.2021.1955844

14 What to avoid and what to think about! Creating effective pre-arrival pages for new and returning students

Michelle Morgan

Pre-arrival pages are an essential tool as colleagues who have contributed to this book have already articulated, as they help bridge the transition into university for students from a variety of backgrounds. They are also invaluable for returners entering a new level of study. This chapter outlines the golden rules I use in creating pre-arrival pages that not only enable engagement but help create a sense of belonging which is a critical ingredient for the retention, progression and success of our students.

My advice is based on 20 years of researching and identifying the stages in the study lifecycle, through talking to students and working with student unions, as well as using my knowledge and experience gained through my various roles in my higher education career that have ranged from administrator to lecturer to learning and teaching coordinator, student experience manager and researcher.

The challenges and what to avoid

The challenges of creating effective pre-arrival pages are many. First, there are the competing demands from all areas of the university who want their information included on the pre-arrival pages even though it may not be relevant for that transition stage. This leads to information overload which can reduce engagement.

Second, it is important to avoid making assumptions about the prior experience of students and what information they need as this can create knowledge and support gaps for different groups of students (e.g. mature, commuters). Higher education has become very diverse so it is essential for an institution to understand their student body so they can identify the key information required and create an effective navigation system for it. For example, there is a misconception that as students may be socially digitally experienced that this extends to their learning, especially post COVID. However, this is not the case as research has started to identify (Morgan, 2023).

DOI: 10.4324/9781003427575-18

Third, it is important to avoid an avalanche of information especially through the provision of a list of links to university processes and systems, which puts the responsibility onto students to access rather than the university.

Fourth, it is important to remember that many incoming students may be viewing the pre-arrival pages on their mobile phone, so it is critical to design information for that platform as well and not just a laptop or PC.

Finally, it is important to avoid marketing led student 'role model' advice and provide 'real' student model advice. The pre-arrival pages are about setting and managing expectations of the reality of university study.

The golden rules of creating engaging pre-arrival pages for students

Below are the four golden rules I use in creating pre-arrival pages. At the heart of pre-arrival pages is providing information that matters, that is clear and that makes a difference.

Golden rule 1: Understanding what information is needed at each stage of the learning journey

Through identifying the stages in the study journey (Morgan, 2011, 2013) and the core themes and activities that need to be considered (see Figure 14.1), the three Ts of information can be provided: Type, appropriate Targeting and Timeliness of information.

This enables key and essential information to be drip fed to students without overloading and overwhelming them. Every student needs to go through these stages and this is particularly important for direct entry students going in to Level 5 and 6/7 where a cohort is already established.

The stages, themes and activities in the Student Experience Transition (SET) model are underpinned by student surveys such as the pre-arrival academic course questionnaire for new students, and the continuation survey for returning students. Both ask students to reflect on their prior learning journey, what they may be concerned about and their expectations for the coming year. This enables the information, advice and guidance to be provided to evolve and adapt to the incoming cohort. The Pandemic and cost-of-living crisis are two examples of changing student concerns and need.

The key stages below should all interlink and should be mapped to the duration of the course.

First contact and admissions

This is where the management of applicant aspirations and expectations of university should start with the provision of clear and honest information.

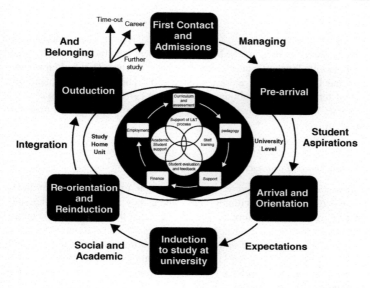

Figure 14.1 Student Experience Transitions Model. More information about the SET model and useful resources can be found by going to: Improving the Student Experience by Michelle Morgan – Official Website www.improving thestudentexperience.com

Pre-arrival (for all students)

This is the stage when new students get ready to come to university, and institutions should have a basic understanding of the backgrounds and support requirements of their new students. It is also when existing students prepare to return to their studies after the vacation period. There are two key elements to pre-arrival which are the hygiene factors (e.g. enrolling and sorting out accommodation), and course information (e.g. knowing when to arrive for course orientation/reorientation, pre-arrival coursework required and support available). Pre-arrival occurs from a few weeks before starting or returning to university study.

Arrival, course orientation and induction to study

Arrival and course orientation is the period when new students arrive on campus, start to navigate their way around an institution and settle into university life (up to three weeks). During the course orientation, students are introduced to their course with 'Induction to study' starting soon afterwards (see next stage). Arrival and Orientation takes place over the first three weeks.

Induction to study

The induction to study stage is where students start to lay the foundations for successful study in their course by equipping them with the relevant study and research skills for the level of study they have entered. This includes identifying and bridging study and knowledge gaps. This stage takes place over the first term/semester enabling students to undertake an 'academic' cycle, so they understand what is required of them and how the learning processes work at university.

Reorientation and reinduction

Reorientation for returners covers information on what is academically expected of them in the coming year, where they can reflect on the skills they acquired the year before, and to identify what they need to build on and develop in order to succeed in their new level of study. Reinduction takes place over a longer period and introduces returning students to new skills to help them actively engage in the learning and assessment processes. The reorientation material resides on a returners' pre-arrival page. Reorientation takes place over a one to two week period.

Outduction

Just as students are inducted into study when they enter higher education, they also need advice and support on how to make the transition out of it so they can effectively adapt to life post study through the outduction stage. This activity should start at the end of the penultimate year of study but proactively be undertaken in the final year. Again, information resides on the final-year pre-arrival pages.

At the heart of my model is the management of expectations and the recognition an understanding that:

- Levels of engagement and sense of belonging will differ between individuals.
- Every individual will have different support requirements which can impact on engagement and a sense of belonging.
- Every individual will have a different perception of what constitutes engagement due to their personal circumstances.
- A high level of engagement does not necessarily result in what is perceived as a successful outcome nor a sense of belonging which I will talk about later. This is dictated by a whole range of reasons including individual characteristics and environment.

Golden rule 2: Understanding and managing the typical pressure points on the pre-arrival pages

The pre-arrival pages should also highlight the typical pressure points that students could experience during each stage along with advice on how to manage these (Morgan, 2020a, 2020b). New students want and need honesty because higher education is a very different experience to school and college, and for returners, the demands for their new level of study will be different to their previous one.

We also need to recognise that for many new students, starting university is a seminal moment in their life. For our young learners, they are moving from a 'child' space to an 'adult' space with all the legal ramifications associated with it. It may be an exciting phase, but the transition is also incredibly stressful due to many areas of their life being disrupted whether that be moving to a new area and sharing accommodation with people they do not know, or learning to be a commuter student alongside those who are not. For students who are care leavers or estranged from their family who have no or limited network of support, this is especially the case.

For returning students, as they have already had the 'lived' experience of university, they often have higher levels of concerns than new students about returning to university and entering the next level of study. And some returners may have taken a year out or undertaken a placement so will be joining a new cohort of students they do not know.

The key to transition success is helping students identify challenges they may experience and plan for it. If a student can see that support has been provided to help their particular situation, this can help them feel that the university cares which helps contribute to a sense of belonging (e.g. Thomas, 2012). Below are some of the typical pressure points that pre-arrival pages can address (Morgan, 2021).

Pre-arrival (for all students)

- Unsure of what to expect at this level of study.
- Knowing what questions to ask at this level of study.
- Worrying about not fitting in.
- Finding accommodation and cost issues.
- Sorting out financial issues such as loans and fee.
- Undertaking pre-enrolment.

Arrival and orientation

- Learning how to study in HE at a specific level.
- Learning how to live with strangers.

- Coping with independence.
- Transition issues such as personal, finance and balancing workloads.
- 'Wobble week'; when students start to question whether this level of study is right for them.
- First assessment and formal feedback.
- Placement activity for courses.
- Coming back after the December break.
- Coping with exams and results at this level of study.
- Dealing with illness or family illness bereavement (non or COVID-19 related).

Induction and reinduction to study

- Reduction in structured learning and scaffolding.
- Increase in independent learning and group assessment.
- Mid-year blues especially for Level 5 as it is a long year.
- End of year exhaustion.
- Coping with workload and assessment that 'counts'.
- University life being different to expectations.
- Relationships with fellow students and staff.
- Anxiety about alternative assessments and the impact on marks.
- Impact on work or placement availability.
- Feeling of the course being poor value for money.
- Balancing work and study.

Preparing to leave – completion or withdrawal students

- Worried about results.
- Worried about sense of failure if did not get the result expected or withdrew early.
- Sense of loss.
- Issues of moving from a structured, safe place to the unknown.
- Loss of direction.
- Challenges with the employment market.
- Family expectations that a university degree will lead to improved chances.
- Uncertainty about how employers will view their degree.

Golden rule 3: Providing meaningful, available and safe advice guidance and support on the pre-arrival pages

If we are to engage new students with key information pre-arrival, that will support arrival and orientation and induction to study transitions, and for returners reorientation, reinduction and outduction, it requires three enabling conditions which are meaningfulness, availability and safety (Kahn, 1990).

Adapting Kahn's model for higher education, the conditions are defined below and contribute to an individual feeling they are accepted and valued by their university, their course staff team and their peers.

Meaningfulness

Every stage should deliver students and staff with clear and meaningful information that provides a clear understanding of what the level of study requires, addresses typical pressure points, and highlights its importance and relevance in terms of the study journey. This helps shape and guide the activity of all stakeholders. Addressing their concerns in an honest and transparent way helps them realise they are not alone.

Safety

By explaining what is required in each stage in the study journey, it sets and manages expectations which in turn provide students and staff with a sense of protection of knowing what to expect, and how to address any challenges they may face.

Availability

By explaining what is expected during each stage, it allows each stakeholder to determine what they need to do and when and plan accordingly. Information needs to be available and accessible both in terms of language and disability. Also critical is the IT platform being used. For example, is it hosted on the internet (public) or intranet (behind the firewall)? Is it linked to the course learning pages? Is it accessible via a mobile phone? This will determine when and how students can access it and the pre-arrival communications that are sent to students.

Golden rule 4: Ensuring that the course is at the heart of system

Once students have obtained advice and undertaken the hygiene activities such as guidance on accommodation and have started the enrolment process, then the course needs to come centre stage.

With pre-arrival course pages, there is often a tendency to have a top down structure which goes from the enrolment process to a welcome by the VC then a welcome by the Dean or Head of school then information about the course. This is too many clicks away from what is central to the students which is their course! Again, we have to be mindful that many students may access information on their mobile phone rather than a PC or laptop. Once a student has enrolled/re-enrolled, it is essential to direct them straight to their dedicated course pre-arrival page. From that page, students can be directed to other core information which I will talk about in a moment.

Meaningfulness

Using the course as the primary distributor of support enables it to appear tailored and bespoke. As a result, students are more likely to engage with the information; therefore, there is a greater opportunity for it to have an impact. Course leaders and their teams are also more likely to engage with centrally produced information and support as they can see the value and meaningfulness of it (Morgan, 2022).

Safety

The pre-arrival course pages should provide a comfortable and safe space with support and assistance where students do not feel intimidated or nervous to ask questions in advance of starting or returning to their course. They should also be encouraged to provide feedback on their experience of using the pre-arrival pages so they can evolve in real time.

Availability

The pre-arrival course pages and the content that should be easily accessible and available can help create and improve relationships between students and course teams, and improve a sense of belonging as it feels personalised.

What to include on the pre-arrival pages

The structure and navigation, to and around the course pre-arrival pages, are critical. It is important for the landing page to contain an enthusiastic welcome from the course leader and the course team and include:

- The date, time and room for the first course welcome and orientation/reorientation session.
- A rationale for and a short list of the information students are expected to engage with for the upcoming level of study such as the course handbook, the general welcome and orientation/reorientation handbook they would have been sent, and any pre-arrival task. Hyperlinks direct to the specified documents or relevant pages containing the information can be provided instead of directing students to look for it via the menu bar.
- A smiling picture of the course leader/Team so it feels welcoming.
- A brief explanation/reminder of how to navigate the pages.

The menu bar, whether top to bottom or left to right, should list the sections of the key information in order of importance along with links for easy access. This can include:

- Detailed course welcome and orientation/reorientation programme.
- Course team and contacts.

- Course handbook (reminder of sections to read).
- Pre-arrival information (including general welcome and orientation handbook, reorientation handbook, international student information).
- Pre-arrival course tasks.
- Course materials.
- Course teaching timetable.
- Top tips for learning (for the relevant level of study).
- Student Union and course rep information.
- Well-being.
- Link to main intranet page.

Each page should have a 'back to the main course page' for ease of access at the start and bottom of the page.

Conclusion

Pre-arrival pages for all students are an essential gateway to the level of learning they are entering, and by evolving the pages to ensure they meet current needs, we have a better chance of engaging our students with the information and helping them feel a sense of belonging.

References

Kahn, W. A. (1990). Psychological conditions of personal engagement and disengagement at work. *Academy of Management Journal*, ProQues, *33*(4), 692–724.

Morgan, M. (Ed.). (2011). *Improving the student experience: The practical guide for universities and colleges*. Routledge.

Morgan, M. (Ed.). (2013). *Supporting student diversity in higher education-a practical guide*. Routledge.

Morgan, M. (2020a). *An exceptional transition to higher education: Induction of new and returning students during the 'new normal' year*. AdvanceHE.

Morgan, M. (2020b, August 3). *Financial concerns and working intentions of incoming Level 4 students -The potential implications for applicants and students in 2020/21 due to Covid19*. www.improvingthestudentexperience. com/library/covid19/Financial_concerns_and_working_intentions_of_ incoming_Level_4_university_students-_implications_of_C19.pdf

Morgan, M. (2022). The student Experience Transitions Model- integrated practice to inspire staff to support students. In D. Nutt & M. McIntosh (Eds.), *The impact of the integrated practitioner in higher education studies in third space professionalism*. Routledge.

Morgan, M. (2023). *Prior learning experience, study expectations and the impact of Covid19 of A-level and BTEC students on entry to university- a three university comparative study*. University of East London.

Thomas, L. (2012). *Building student engagement and belonging in higher education at a time of change*. Paul Hamlyn Foundation.

Index

Note: Page numbers in *italics* indicate a figure and page numbers in **bold** indicate a table on the corresponding page.